FF-1
9365
5   13

Introduction

As a Student Naval Aviator I happened to be in the right place at the right time. In 1986, I was in the middle of flight school in Pensacola, Florida. It was the 75th Anniversary of naval aviation, and on top of that, the movie "Top Gun" had just been released.

Go back fifty-five years to 1941, and picture young men with their minds on the air, watching Pathe film clips from the air war in Europe just before the feature film starring Ralph Bellamy, Fred McMurray and Erroll Flynn. The movie, of course, was "Dive Bomber" and I cannot help but think that young men of that era made up their minds to be Navy pilots inspired by the classic lines of Fred McMurray's Grumman F3F-2.

On 10 October 1941, VMF-211 turned in its last Grumman F3F-2, bringing the era of the biplane as a front-line fighter platform to a close. It was a mere ten years earlier,when Grumman Aircraft Engineering Corporation's first aircraft, the XFF-1, took to the air, ushering in the era of all-metal monocoque construction, enclosed cockpits and retractable landing gear for Navy aircraft.

As airframe manufacturers go, the Grumman Engineering Corporation came on the scene much later than most, incorporating on 6 December 1929. Grumman's first two designs, the G-1 and G-2, weren't even aircraft, but amphibious aircraft floats, designated the Model A and Model B floats respectively. Eight Model A floats and fifteen Model B floats were were purchased by the U.S. Navy between 1930 and 1932. Fitted to Vought 02Us and O3Us, the floats were of monocoque aluminum construction with retractable landing gear.

Grumman Design 3 (G-3) was never built. It was to have been a twin engined amphibious monoplane similar in appearance to the Consolidated P2Y series and was intended for use by the Coast Guard. Grumman's second aircraft design, the G-4, was a small amphibious single engine biplane and was proposed for use by the U.S.. Army Air Corps as an observation aircraft, but like the G-3 before it, was never built.

XFF-1

In February of 1930, during the discussions that led to the purchase of eight Grumman Model A floats, the U.S. Navy Bureau of Aeronautics (BuAer) asked Grumman about the feasibility of adopting their patented landing gear retraction mechanism to existing fighter aircraft such as the Boeing F4B series. Grumman was doubtful about the success of such modifications, and additionally, did not want to see another manufacturer benefit from Grumman technical expertise. Coupled with a forthcoming Navy requirement for a new two seat shipboard fighter, Grumman submitted a proposal to BuAer on 10 March 1930, for Grumman Design 5 (G-5) known initially as the High Performance Two Seat Fighter (HPTSF).

The G-5 design was a radical departure from state-of-the-art shipboard aircraft of the time, incorporating an enclosed cockpit with dual sliding canopies, fully retractable main landing gear and most importantly, all-metal construction. The fuselage was to be of semi-monocoque aluminum alloy construction. The wing structure was also aluminum, but was to be covered with fabric. Power was provided by a single 575 hp Wright R-1820-E Cyclone air-cooled radial engine turning a two blade ground adjustable propeller. Grumman's performance estimates showed the aircraft to perform better than any fighter in Naval service at the time. Skeptical of the estimates, BuAer requested a set of drawings from which they could construct a wind tunnel model of the aircraft. It wasn't until nearly a year later that the Navy obtained a

The XFF-1 (BuNo 8878) rests on blocks while the flotation bags in the upper wings are tested. The fabric has not been applied to either wing surface and the landing gear is retracted. (NMNA)

The XFF-1 in its original configuration on a test flight near NAS Anacostia on 4 February 1932. The performance of the two-seat XFF-1 was better than any single seat fighter in the Navy inventory and the Navy ordered twenty-seven aircraft on 19 December 1932. (Grumman)

Grumman Biplane Fighters

in action

By LCDR Richard S. Dann, USNR

Color by Don Greer

Illustrated by Joe Sewell & Ernesto Cumpian

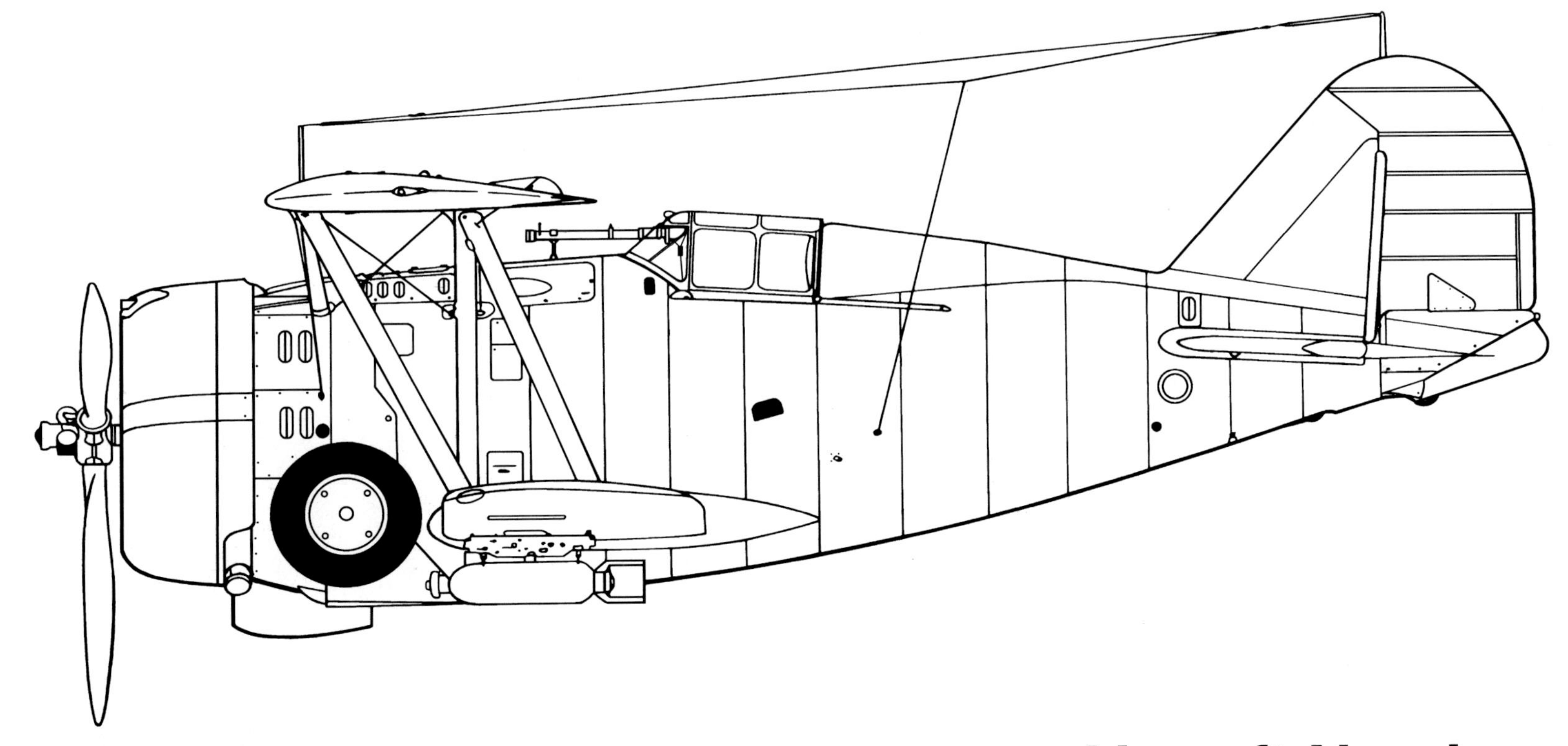

Aircraft Number 160

squadron/signal publications

An F3F-2 of VF-6 aboard USS ENTERPRISE (CV-6) engages Army Air Corps P-26As camouflaged in temporary water colors during war games over Hawaii in May of 1939.

Acknowledgements

I want to thank everyone who assisted me on this project, with articles and tidbits of information. Special thanks go to Roger Seybel at the Grumman History Center and Jim Curry at the National Museum of Naval Aviation. Without the help of these two gentlemen, I would not have been able to complete this book. The following people and organizations contributed to this project:

William J. Armstrong	Richard S. Allen	Peter M. Bowers
Jack Binder	Sid Bradd	Tony & Marty Bunch
Burl Burlingame	John M. Campbell	Don Connolly
Allison Dann	Dave & Mike Dann	Fred C. Dickey Jr.
Archie DiFante	Jeff Ethell	Ron Williamson
Jerry Farrell	Gary Fisk	AAHS
Rene Francillion	Hill Goodspeed	Air International
BGEN Robert Galer, USMC (Ret)	COL Ole C. Griffith, USAF (Ret}	
COL Milo Haines, USMC (Ret)	William T. Larkins	Cinema Air Inc.
Amanda Sproles Dann	Bob Lawson	Ray Wagner
D.K. Lindeman	Dave Lucabaugh	Grumman Corporation
Dick Martin	CAPT Ed McKellar, USN, (Ret)	
William L. Swisher	National Museum of Naval Aviation (NMNA)	
Nicholas J. Waters III	Mrs. Alice Williams	McGuire's Irish Pub
Campbell Archives/OKC	CAPT W.E. Scarborough, USN (Ret)	
National Aviation Museum of Canada (NAMC)		
San Diego Aerospace Museum (SDAM)		
Tailhook Association		

ISBN 0-89747-353-1

If you have any photographs of aircraft, armor, soldiers or ships of any nation, particularly wartime snapshots, why not share them with us and help make Squadron/Signal's books all the more interesting and complete in the future. Any photograph sent to us will be copied and the original returned. The donor will be fully credited for any photos used. Please send them to:

Squadron/Signal Publications, Inc.
1115 Crowley Drive
Carrollton, TX 75011-5010

Если у вас есть фотографии самолётов, вооружения, солдат или кораблей любой страны, особенно, снимки времён войны, поделитесь с нами и помогите сделать новые книги издательства Эскадрон/Сигнал ещё интереснее. Мы переснимем ваши фотографии и вернём оригиналы. Имена приславших снимки будут сопровождать все опубликованные фотографии. Пожалуйста, присылайте фотографии по адресу:

Squadron/Signal Publications, Inc.
1115 Crowley Drive
Carrollton, TX 75011-5010

軍用機、装甲車両、兵士、軍艦などの写真を所持しておられる方は いらっしゃいませんか？どの国のものでも結構です。作戦中に撮影されたものが特に良いのです。Squadron/Signal社の出版する刊行物において、このような写真は内容を一層充実し、興味深くすることができます。当方にお送り頂いた写真は、複写の後お返しいたします。出版物中に写真を使用した場合は、必ず提供者のお名前を明記させて頂きます。お写真は下記にご送付ください。

Squadron/Signal Publications, Inc.
1115 Crowley Drive
Carrollton, TX 75011-5010

Dedication:

I would like to dedicate this book to the memory of my parents, Jim and Mary Dann, in whom I am well pleased. I miss them. Also, to my daughters Allison and Ashley who are a constant source of amazement and inspiration to me. I love you girls, "bigger than the sky!"

A FF-1 of Fighting Five (VF-5B) lands aboard USS LEXINGTON (CV-2) during 1934. The Red Rippers markings are some of the oldest in the Navy (currently being carried by VF-11, flying F-14Ds). The tail markings were True Blue and the section markings were Willow Green. (Grumman)

cost estimate for the construction of a prototype, and, on 28 March 1931, ordered a single prototype of the G-5, under the Navy designation, XFF-1.

Construction of the XFF-1 (BuN0 8878) was begun shortly afterward at Grumman's small factory in Baldwin, Long Island, New York. Guaranteed delivery of the aircraft in mid-October could not be achieved, primarily due to the company's relocation to a more suitable production facility on Curtiss Field in Valley Stream, Long Island, during November of 1931. The XFF-1 took to the air for the first time on 29 December 1931, two and a half months behind schedule and was delivered to NAS Anacostia the same day. The 575 hp R-1820-E gave the XFF-1 a top speed of 195 mph; which was seven mph faster than the Boeing F4B-2, which was currently the front-line fighter in the Navy inventory.

Following delivery to Anacostia, the aircraft began Board of Inspection and Survey (BIS) trials. BIS evaluators recommended several changes to the XFF-1 and these included a redesigned canopy with less framing, beefed up landing gear struts and the deletion of accessory cooling vents on the forward engine access panels. In May of 1932, the aircraft was flown back to Valley Stream to be re-engined with a 750 hp Wright R-1820-78 radial engine, which boosted top speed to 201 mph. The XFF-1 carried an armament of two forward firing .30 caliber machine guns and a single .30 caliber machine gun on a swivel mount in the rear cockpit.

After the satisfactory completion of tests at Anacostia, the Navy ordered twenty-seven production aircraft on 19 December 1932, under the designation FF-1 (BuNos 9350-9376).

The XFF-1 was flown back to Grumman to bring the aircraft up to production standards. External mass balances were added to the ailerons and the engine cooling shield was removed. Once these changes were made, the aircraft lost the "X" designation. The aircraft was then sent to the West Coast where it served with VF-5S and then with VF-5B. In January of 1934, the aircraft was sent back to Anacostia, where it remained, except for short periods, until it was stricken on 31 March 1937.

During the Summer of 1936, the XFF-1 was involved in Project YEHUDI, which studied the effects of illumination as a form of camouflage. 12, 600 candlepower landing lights were attached to the XFF-1 which were pointed away from the aircraft and at the potential observer. Test flights in October 1936, proved to be disappointing. Later experiments during the Second World War, on USAAF B-24s and Navy TBF-1s, successfully proved the YEHUDI concept was practical.

The Navy requested several modifications to the XFF-1 prototype after it completed the Board of Inspection and Survey trials. These included a modified canopy with reduced framing and deletion of the cooling vents on the forward fuselage. (Grumman)

Prototype Development

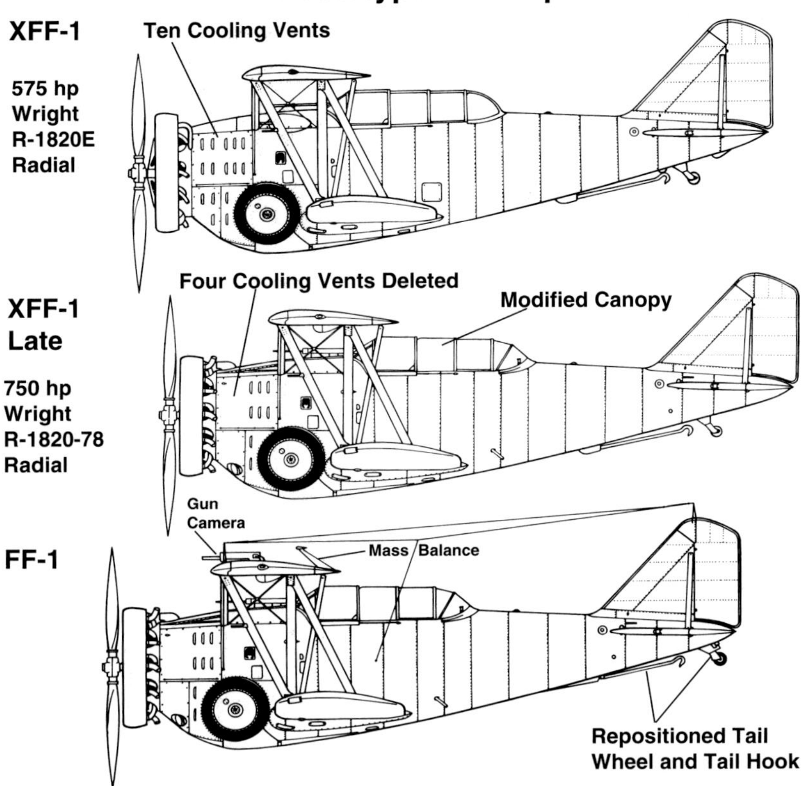

The XFF-1 was modified to production standards and the X dropped from its designation. The aircraft had mass balances added to the ailerons and the engine cooling shield was deleted. After finishing BIS trials at NAS Anacostia, the aircraft was transferred to VF-5B for a short tour. The prototype finished its career back at NAS Anacostia. (NMNA)

Development

XFF-1

FF-1

FF-2

G-23

XF2F-1

F2F-1

XF3F-1

F3F-1

XF3F-2

F3F-2

F3F-3

G-32

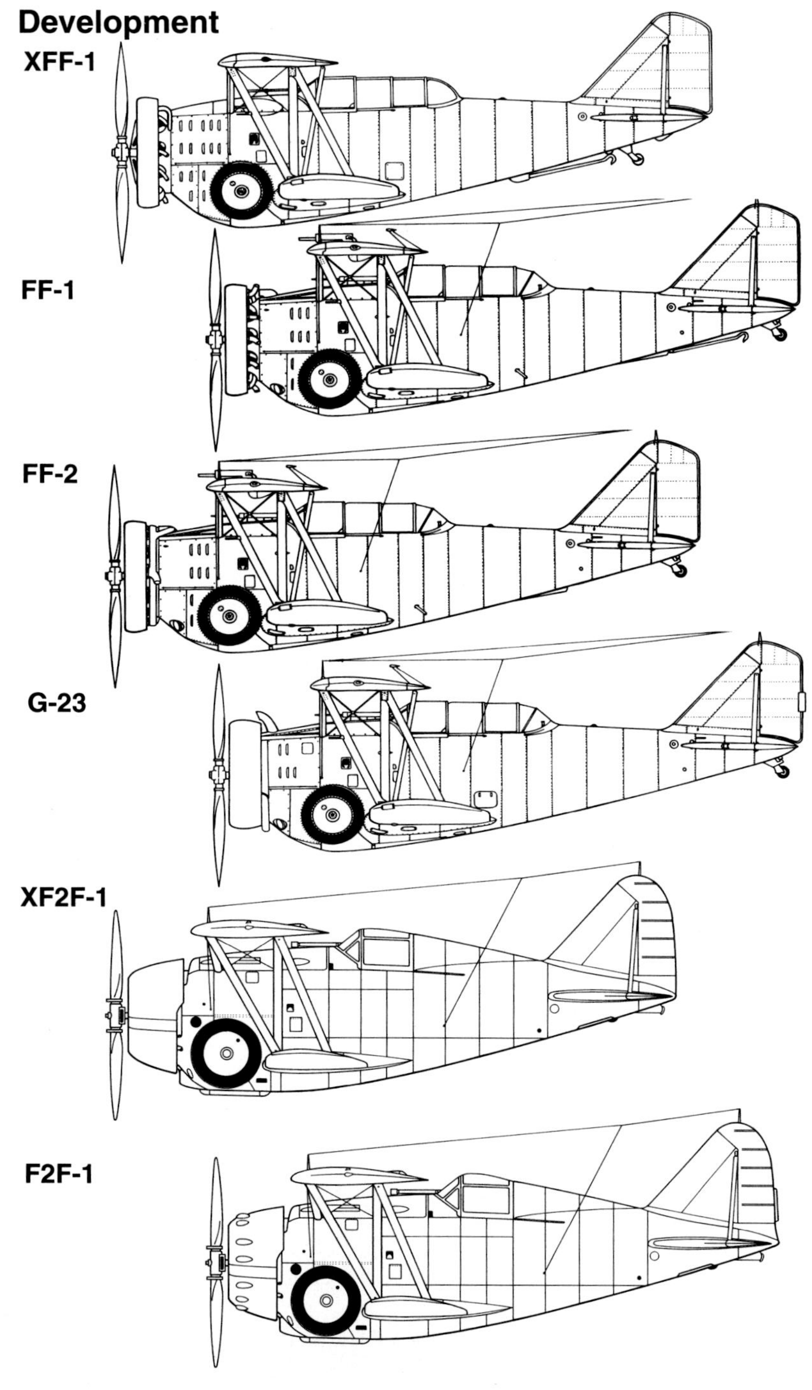

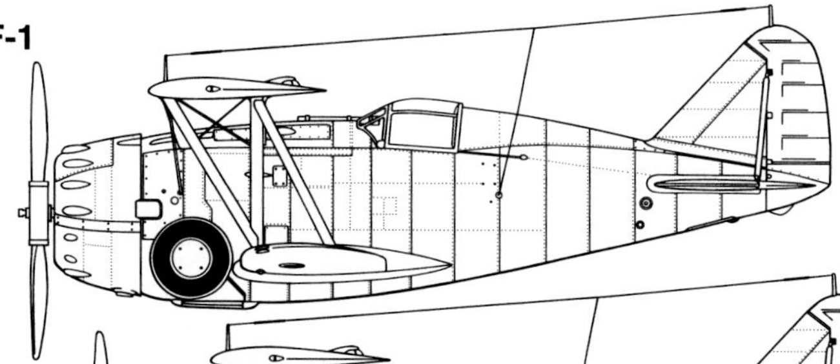

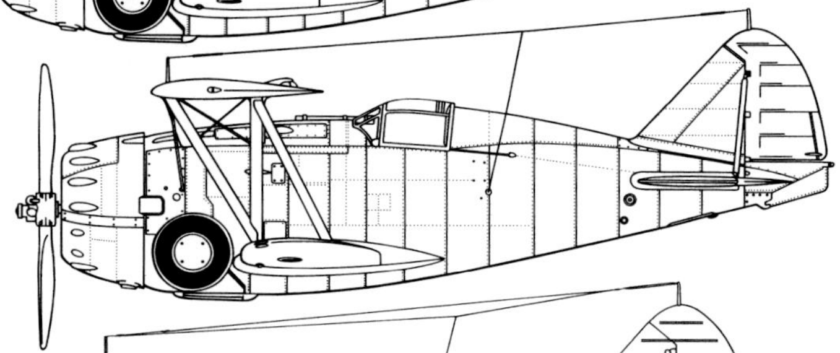

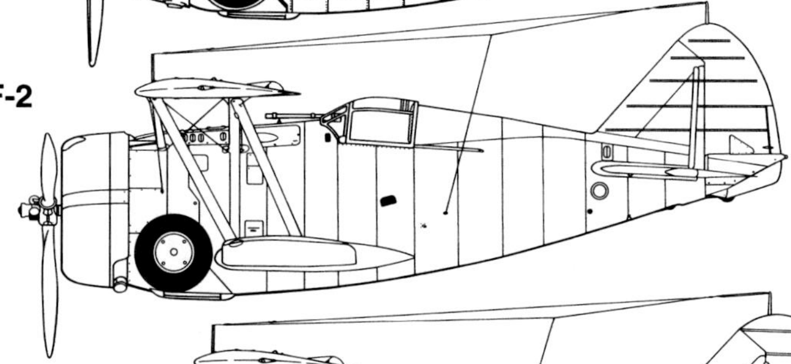

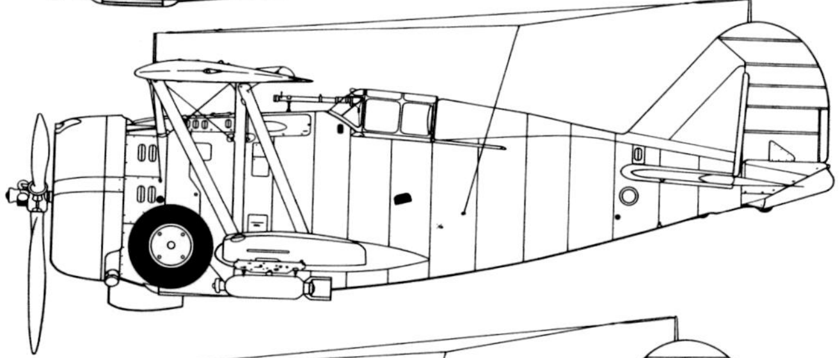

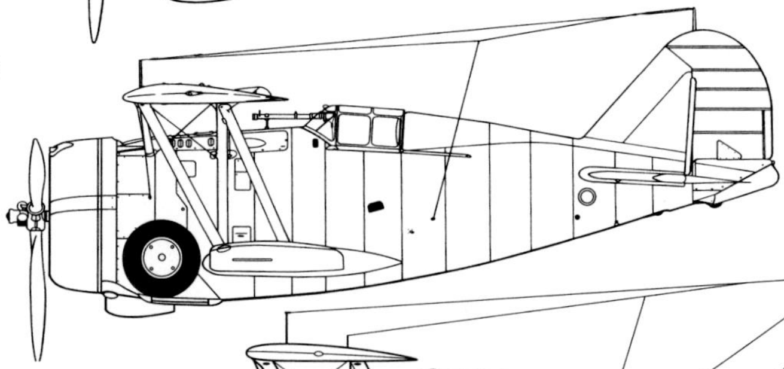

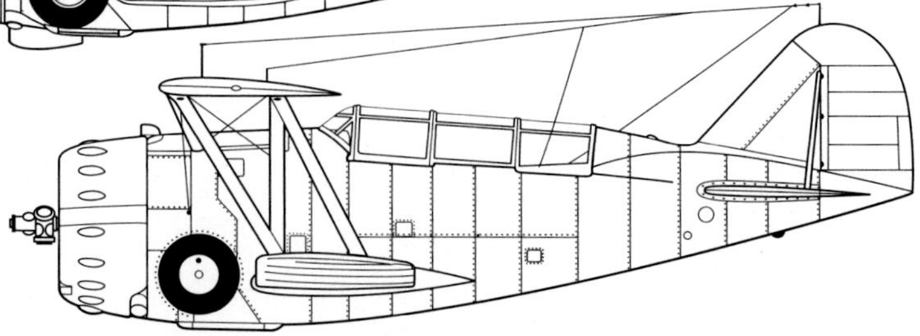

FF-1

The production FF-1 differed from the late prototype mainly in the position of the tail wheel and arresting hook. The tail wheel was moved back under the rudder and the tailhook was also repositioned further to the rear.

Deliveries of the twenty-seven production aircraft commenced in April of 1933, with the last aircraft being delivered in November of 1933. VF-5B was the only squadron to completely equip with the type, initially receiving twenty-five of the twenty-seven aircraft. VF-1B received a single production aircraft (BuNo 9376) as did NAS Anacostia (BuNo 9350).

VF-5B took their aircraft aboard USS LEXINGTON (CV-2). In the Fall of 1935, VF-5B was reassigned to USS RANGER (CV-4). Then, in November of 1935 VF-5B turned in nine of their FF-1s and received nine F2F-1s. The squadron operated both types until they could be replaced by F3F-1s in March and April of 1936. This ended front-line use of the FF-1. As the aircraft were withdrawn from front line service, twenty-two of the remaining twenty-five aircraft were converted to FF-2s by the Naval Aircraft Factory in Philadelphia.

Canopy Modification

XFF-1

XFF-1 (Late) & FF-1

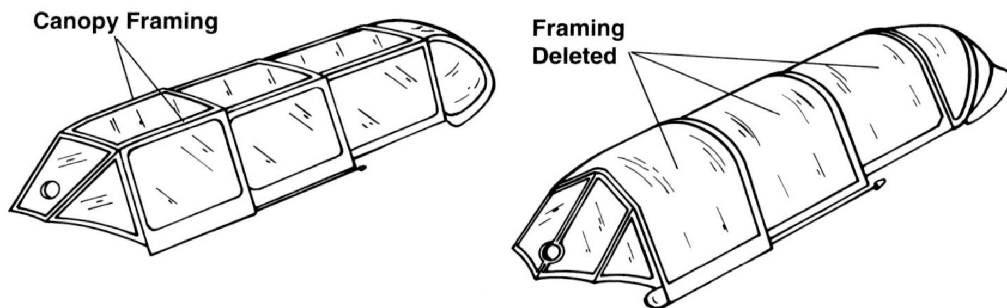

FF-1s of VF-5B fly in line abreast formation during 1934. All three aircraft carry a White Battle E marking on the fuselage below the windshield and have Red section markings. Each aircraft also has a gun camera mounted on the upper wing center section. VF-5B served aboard both the USS LEXINGTON (CV-2) and USS RANGER (CV-4). (NMNA)

FF-1s of VF-5B during August of 1934. The three aircraft in the background make up the sixth section and have Lemon Yellow section markings. The aircraft in the foreground (BuNo 9365) had Willow Green section markings. This aircraft was later converted to FF-2 standards and crashed while attached to NRAB Minneapolis during September of 1938. (Grumman)

Ff-1 (BuNo 9361) of Fighting Five (VF-5B). The section colors were Black and the tail surfaces were True Blue with White lettering. The fuselage cut-out for the adjustable horizontal stabilizer is visible just behind the round inspection plate. The purpose of the wire coming out of the rear cockpit is unknown. BuNo 9361 was destroyed in February of 1935 while in transit to the East Coast. (Peter Bowers)

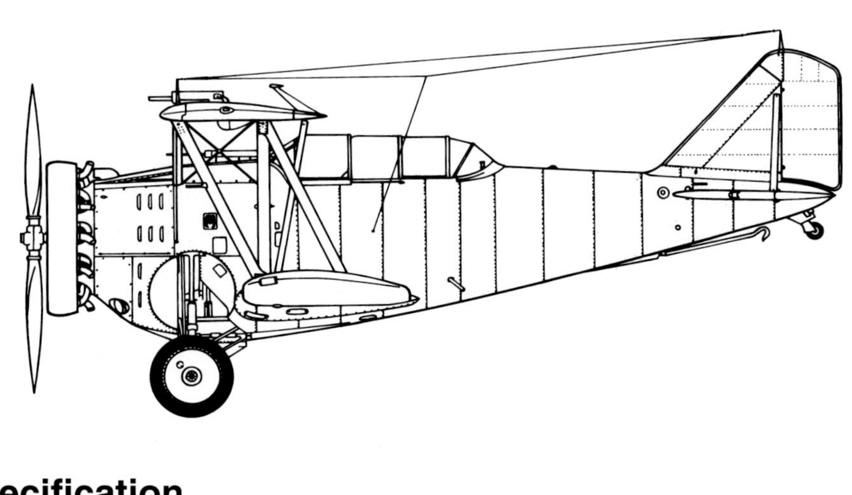

Specification

Grumman FF-1

Wingspan..34 feet 6 inches (10.5 m**)**
Length..24 feet 6 inches (7.46 m**)**
Height...11 feet 1 inch (3.35 m)
Empty Weight...................................3,076 pounds (1,395.2 kg)
Maximum Weight................................4,655 pounds (2,111.5 kg)

Powerplant...One 750 hp Wright R-1820-78 Cyclone
    air-cooled radial engine
Armament..Two forward fiiring.30 caliber machine guns
    and one .30 caliber machine gun in rear
    cockpit.
Speed..207 mph (333.1 kph)
Service Ceiling.................................22,400 feet (6,827.5 m)
Range..732 miles (1,178 km)
Crew..Two

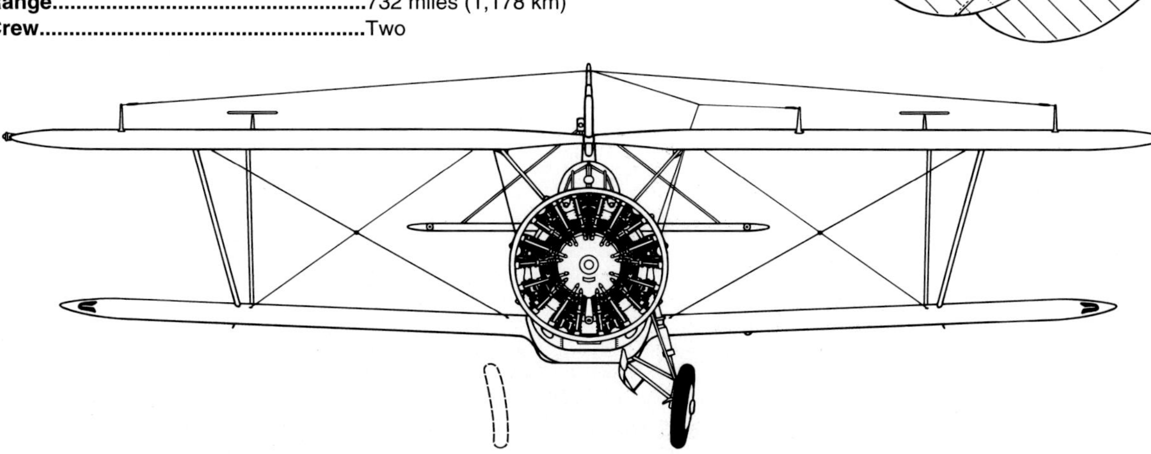

This FF-1 (BuNo 9355) of Fighting Five on the ramp at NAS Long Beach, California, was assigned to the USS LEXINGTON (CV-2). It carried Lemon Yellow section markings and a True Blue tail. The aircraft has a gun camera mounted on the upper wing. This FF-1 ended its career at NAS Jacksonville, FL. (Ed McCallom via W. L. Swisher)

A FF-1 on the ramp at NAS North Island, California on 25 January 1934. The aircraft had True Blue section markings and tail surfaces and the fuselage was Light Gray. The aircraft was flown by Ensign Corliss and his name was painted on the fuselage under the canopy rail. VF-5B received twenty-five of the twenty-seven FF-1s built. This aircraft was last assigned to NAS Norfolk, VA, before being retired. (National Archives via Dave Lucabaugh)

A ground crewman prepares to start the engine of this FF-1 (BuNo 9367). This aircraft was later converted to FF-2 standards and was the last serviceable FF-2. The fighter was finally stricken from the inventory while assigned to Base Air Detachment One at Marine Corps Air Station Quantico, Virginia. (Larkins)

FF-2

Upon withdrawal from fleet service in 1935, twenty-two of the remaining twenty-five FF-1s were sent to the Naval Aircraft Factory in Philadelphia for modification and upgrading. Upon completion of these modifications the aircraft were redesignated as FF-2s and delivered to various Naval and Marine Corps reserve units across the United States.

Intended for use as fighter-trainers, the modifications made to the FF-1s included to the installation of dual flight controls, the removal of the tailhook and the installation of an engine exhaust collector ring in place of individual exhaust stacks used on the FF-1. Additionally, carburetor heat was bled off the exhaust collector ring. Finally, an HF/RDF radio was installed, and a five stranded loop antenna was installed between the upper and lower starboard wings. Although intended to be a trainer, the FF-2s retained their full armament.

Once brought up to FF-2 standard, the twenty-two FF-2s were distributed to the following Naval Reserve Air Bases (NRAB):

NRAB	Quantity	Squadron
Philadelphia	1	VN-5RD4 (USNR)
Glenview	5	VN-10RD9 (USNR)
Grosse Isle	4	VN-9RD9 (USNR) VO-5MR/SS-2MR (USMCR)
Minneapolis	3	VN-11RD9 (USNR) VO-6MR (USMCR)
Robertson, MO	3	VN-12RD9 (USNR)
Kansas City	6	VN-17RD9 (USNR) VO-10MR (USMCR)

By June 1940, only fifteen FF-2s were still flying with reserve units, these being used by NRABs Chicago, Detroit, Minneapolis, St. Louis and Kansas City. Each unit had three aircraft. By December of 1941, only seven were left. The last FF-2 was stricken in July of 1942 after serving with Base Air Detachment One at MCAS Quantico, Virginia.

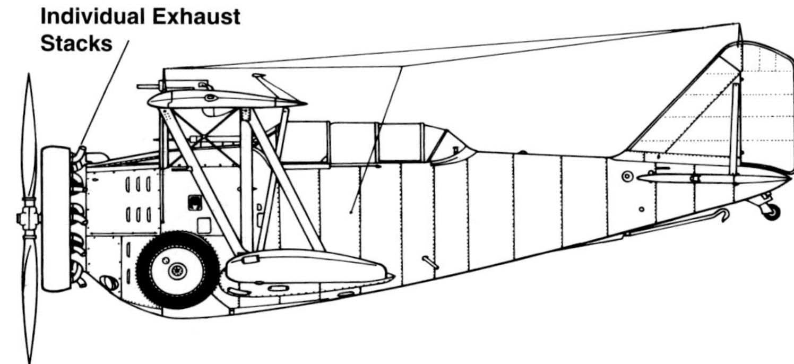

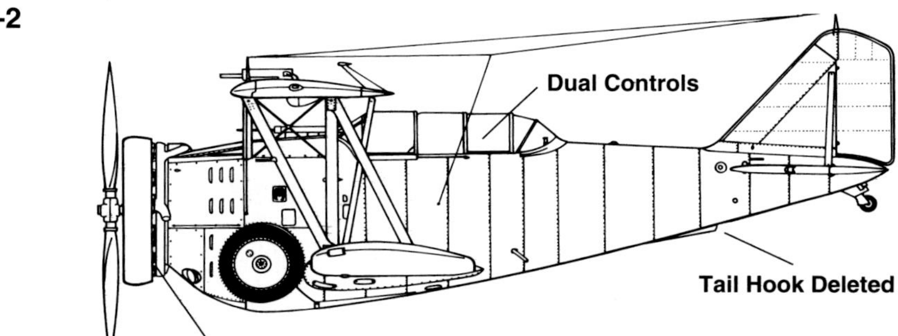

A FF-2 (BuNo 9359) chocked on the grass at (probably) Chicago during 1938. The tail surfaces and cowling were Red. The aircraft had the tail hook removed for operations from land bases. (Vernon Jacobson via W. L. Swisher)

This FF-2 at the Alleghany County Airport has the Navy/Marine Reserve insignia on the fuselage. One of the modifications done to the FF-1s to bring them up to FF-2 standards was the addition of an exhaust collector ring in place of the individual exhaust stacks on the FF-1. The aircraft appears to have a Red cowling and tail surfaces. (Jack Binder)

This FF-2 (BuNo 9367) was assigned to Base Air Detachment One at MCAS Quantico, Virginia, and made a belly landing on 6 May 1942. The Marine Corps emblem was carried on the fuselage just below the front cockpit. The aircraft had a rear view mirror attached to the left forward fuselage cabane strut. (Tailhook Photo Service)

An unmarked FF-2 (BuNo 9365) at the Allegheny County Airport. Once the twenty-five FF-1s were retired from active service, twenty-two were sent to the Naval Aircraft Factory in Philadelphia for modification to FF-2 standards. This FF-2 was equipped with a HF radio used for radio direction finding. There is a five strand antenna running between the upper and lower wing just behind the outboard N strut. (Jack Binder)

Two FF-2s share the flight line with three Berliner Joyce OJ-2s at the Allegheny County Airport, PA. The section colors for reserve units generally were the same as fleet units. These aircraft have Insignia Red section markings. The chevrons on the upper wings of all five aircraft point forward. (Jack Binder)

This FF-2 was the second production FF-1 (BuNo 9351) and had previously served as the commanding officer's aircraft in VF-5B. FF-2s differed from the FF-1 in having the tailhook deleted, dual flight controls and a exhaust collector ring in place of the earlier individual exhaust stacks. (Jeff Ethell)

SF-1

On 9 June 1931, the Navy ordered a single prototype for a scout aircraft based on the basic FF-1 airframe under the designation XSF-1. Externally similar to the XFF-1, the XSF-1 was slightly modified to configure it for the scouting role. To increase maximum range, one of the forward firing .30 caliber guns was removed and an additional forty-five gallons of fuel were to be carried for an extended loiter time.

It took Grumman a lengthy fourteen months to fly the XSF-1 prototype. This was partly due to the company moving from its tiny Baldwin, Long Island facility to a more satisfactory location at a factory in Valley Stream, New York. The first flight of the XSF-1 (BuNo 8940) occurred on 20 August 1932. Ten days after the first flight, the XSF-1 was flown to Naval Air Station Anacostia to begin Service Acceptance Trials. The XSF-1 remained on strength until 1938, when it was stricken from the records of serviceable aircraft.

The XSF-1 was powered by a 750 hp Wright R-1820-78 Cyclone air-cooled radial engine enclosed in a Townend ring cowling similar to the installation on the XFF-1. Like the FF-1, the XSF-1 had individual exhaust stubs for each cylinder, a feature that would be deleted on the production aircraft in favor of an exhaust collector ring. The engine drove a two blade, nine foot six diameter Hamilton Standard ground adjustable propeller. The airframe was of all-metal semi-monocoque construction while the wings were also constructed of aluminum, but were fabric covered. The horizontal tail surfaces and all control surfaces were of all-metal construction. The XSF-1 also had adjustable stabilizers with a -1 to +5 degree range of travel. The XSF-1 had external aileron mass balances like those used on the FF-1, although production SF-1s did not use them.

Sufficiently satisfied with the performance of the XSF-1 during acceptance trials at NAS Anacostia, BuAer ordered thirty-four production variants (BuNos 9460-9493) under the designation SF-1. As with any aircraft transitioning from prototype to production, airframe changes were made. Production FF-1s featured a longer-chord NACA cowling, a variable pitch propeller and an exhaust collector ring in place of the individual exhaust stubs. Initially the SF-1 was powered by a Wright R-1820-78 engine, although later aircraft in the production run were re-engined with the 750 hp Wright R-1820-84 air-cooled radial. In an effort to reduce drag, the external mass balances used on the ailerons of the prototype, were replaced by internal mass balance weights. With these aerodynamic refinements, the SF-1 was five

XSF-1 (BuNo 8940) had a polished Aluminum airframe with Chrome Yellow upper wing tops. The XSF-1 used external mass balances on the ailerons which were deleted on the production aircraft. (W. L. Swisher)

Development

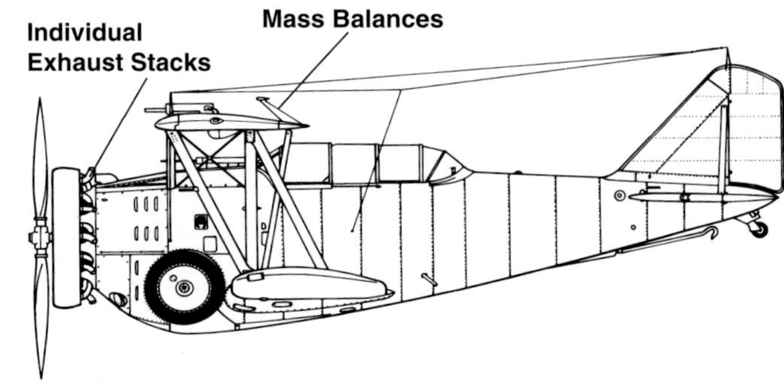

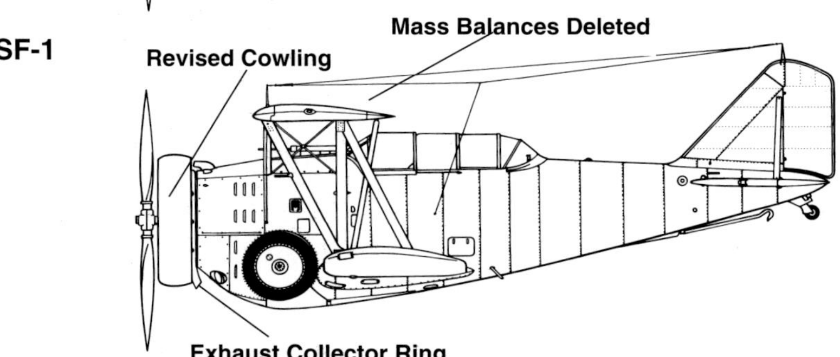

mph faster than the FF-1 with a top speed of 206 mph.

Initial deliveries to the fleet commenced on 15 February 1934, and ended on 12 July 1934 with the delivery of the thirty-third SF-1. The production contract was modified, and the thirty-fourth aircraft was converted to serve as the XSF-2 prototype. Only one squadron completely re-equipped with SF-1s, Scouting Three (VS-3B) aboard the USS LEXINGTON (CV-2). Five fighter squadrons each took delivery of a single SF-1, these squadrons being VF-1B,

The first production SF-1 was delivered to Bombing Two (VB-2B) for the utility/scout role, and carried no section markings. The unit was assigned to the USS SARATOGA (CV-3) and had Insignia Red tail surfaces. The aircraft in the background is a Curtiss BFC-2. (Fred C. Dickey Jr.)

A SF-1 (BuN0 9484) at NRAB Long Beach, California during 1935. This aircraft carried the markings of the second section leader of Scouting Three (VS-3B) and had White section markings and Lemon Yellow tail surfaces. Later the aircraft was assigned to NAS Jacksonville, FL and was stricken on 1 May 1941. (Ed McCollom via W. L. Swisher)

VF-2B, VF-3B, VF-5B and VF-6B. Additionally Bombing Two and Bombing Five received single aircraft. These SF-1s served as squadron liaison aircraft, and were also used to handle navigation and communications during squadron movements. After little more than a year, the SF-1 series was withdrawn from front-line service and distributed to units of the Navy and Marine Air Reserve. The following NRABs received SF-1s:

NRAB	Quantity	Squadron
Brooklyn	4	VN-3RD3/VN4RD3 (USNR) VO-2MR (USMCR)
Anacostia	4	VN-6R (USNR) VO-JMR (USMCR)
Long Beach	6	VN-13RD11/VN-16RD11 (USNR) VO-7MR(USMCR)
Oakland	7	VN-14RD12 (USNR) VO-8MR (USMCR)
Seattle	5	VN-1SRD13 (USNR) VO-9MR/SS-3MR (USMCR)

By December of 1941, eleven SF-1s remained on strength. Once stricken from the inventory, these aircraft were used as ground instructional airframes until they were scrapped.

SF-1 (BuNo 9490) was assigned to VF-3B during 1935 and deployed aboard USS RANGER (CV-4) with Willow Green tail surfaces. Aircraft with side numbers 19 and above did not carry section markings. The aircraft was fitted with a five strand HF radio antenna between the wings. (Campbell Archives/OKC)

A SF-1 (BuNo 9463) parked at the Union Air Terminal, Burbank, California. This was the only SF-1 assigned to VF-6B and served as a utility aircraft before being transferred to NRAB Long Beach for use by both the Navy and Marine Reserve units based there. It was lost on 11 August 1939, when it crashed and burned. (W. L. Swisher)

A flight of three SF-1s assigned to NRAB Oakland, California in echelon formation. Both Navy and Marine Corps reserve units flew these aircraft on alternating weekends. The aircraft have had the wheel covers painted to match their section colors. The leader has Red section markings; while the others had White section markings. (NMNA)

GG-1

During 1934 Grumman built a single GG-1 (X12V) for use as company demonstrator. Built from unused components from both FF-1 and SF-1 production, the GG-1 flew for the first time on 28 September 1934.

The GG-1 differed from both the FF-1 and the SF-1 in having a 450 hp Pratt & Whitney R-1340 engine. The new engine necessitated a redesign of the forward fuselage, and the aircraft was fitted with a new cowling featuring blisters over the rocker arms. Additionally, the GG-1 incorporated a streamlined upper rear fuselage decking in place of a hinged rear canopy. The aircraft was painted overall Red with Black trim, becoming the first "Red Ship" used by the company. Grumman operated this aircraft until October of 1936, when the aircraft was returned to the factory for modification. Modifications to the aircraft included the installation of an 890 hp Wright R-1820-F52 engine and a controllable pitch propeller. The streamlined fairing on the upper rear fuselage decking was removed, and a standard FF-1/SF-1 canopy was installed.

In November of 1936, the modified GG-1 was sold to the Canadian Car & Foundry test pilot Howard Klein for use as the G-23 demonstrator. Earlier in the year the CC&F Board of Directors had decided to open the Fort William, Ontario, assembly plant for the manufacture of aircraft and obtained a license to produce the export variant of the FF-1/SF-1 series, Grumman Design 23, or G-23. On 20 November 1936, Howard Klein took delivery of the GG-1 (now registered as NR12V) and flew it to Montreal. On 15 December, the aircraft was flown back to the U.S., to Floyd Bennent Field, New York, for demonstration to the Spanish Republican government purchasing commission.

In an effort to solicit orders for the G-23, Howard Klein embarked on a sales tour of Latin America, entering Mexico on 17 March 1937. An order was placed for one G-23 by the Nicaraguan government. Discussions were held with the Mexican government regarding the possible manufacture of G-23s in Mexico and G-23 (CC&F c/n 148) was eventually delivered to Mexico. The discussions ended with no other orders being placed. On 15 June 1937, the

The GG-1 (X12V) was powered by a 450 hp Pratt & Whitney R-1340 air-cooled radial; which made it necessary to redesign the forward fuselage and cowling. The aircraft also differed from the FF-1/SF-1 in having a longer canopy faired into the fuselage decking. The aircraft was overall "Cornell Red" with Black trim. (Grumman)

The modified GG-1 at Floyd Bennett Field, New York in December of 1936. The aircraft was re-engined with a 890 hp Wright R-1820-F52 air-cooled radial, giving it a top speed of 242 mph. As part of its rebuild, the aircraft was also fitted with split flaps on the upper wing. During March of 1937, the aircraft embarked on a sales tour of Latin America and was lost at sea off the Nicaraguan coast on 29 September 1937. (NAMC)

aircraft suffered a minor accident in Mexico City. The aircraft was lost at sea on 29 September 1937, after running out of fuel near San Juan Del Norte, Nicaragua, thus ending the career of the GG-1.

G-23

In June of 1936, the Canadian Car & Foundry obtained the rights to assemble G-23 aircraft at its Fort William, Ontario plant. Under the agreement worked out between CC&F and Grumman, fifty-two G-23 fuselages were manufactured by Grumman and shipped to Canada. Additionally, seventy wing assemblies and sixty-six sets of tails were manufactured by Brewster and also sent to CC&F.

Production G-23s differed very little from the remanufactured GG-1. The G-23 was powered by a 890 hp Wright R-1820-F52 engine turning a Hamilton Standard controllable pitch propeller. An eighteen inch-chord NACA cowling similar to that used on the SF-1 was installed on the G-23. Armament consisted of two forward firing .30 caliber machine guns with an additional .30 caliber gun on a flexible mount in the rear cockpit. The G-23 also had provisions for two 110 pound bombs, one under each wing.

Japan

The second G-23 (CC&F construction number 102) was purchased by the Imperial Japanese Navy to evaluate the landing gear technology of the aircraft. The aircraft was, designated as the AXG1, the short designation for "Navy Experimental Type Carrier Fighter." The aircraft made its first flight on 12 February 1938, and was delivered to Japan later that month. Repeated inquiries as to the disposition of this aircraft have proved unsuccessful.

Nicaragua

Nicaragua was the recipient of the first G-23 (CC&F construction number 101) for its fledgling air force, *Fuzera Aerea de la Guardia National de Nicaragua*. First flown on 3 February 1938, the aircraft was delivered to Nicaragua in June. Little is known about the service history of this aircraft, and it was scrapped by the Nicaraguan Air Force in 1942 at Zolodan airfield in Managua.

The aircraft sat in the scrapyard until 1961, when it was discovered by American crop-dusting pilot, J.R. Sirmons. Purchasing the aircraft, Sirmons transported the remains to Chinandega, Nicaragua. During the next four winters, Sirmons and his family and friends restored the aircraft to flying condition. Unable to refurbish the original R-1820 engine, Sirmons located a 600 hp Pratt & Whitney R-1340 engine and fitted it to the airframe. In addition, a three-blade Hamilton Standard propeller was used in place of the original two-blade unit. Restoration was completed in February of 1966 and the aircraft was readied for its 2,100 mile flight to Sirmon's home town of Atoka, Oklahoma. As a precaution, Sirmons installed sheet metal fairings over the landing gear wells and elected to fly the aircraft to the United States with the landing gear extended.

Once back in the United States, Sirmons was invited to fly his G-23 (N2803J) to the Grumman facility at Peconic, Long Island for the Twentieth Anniversary of the Blue Angels. Shortly after this, Grumman purchased the aircraft and restored it to represent a FF-l (BuNo 9358) as flown by the Commanding Officer of VF-5B, the "Red Rippers."

Following the restoration, it was decided that the aircraft would be donated to the Naval Aviation Museum at NAS Pensacola, Florida. On 9 June 1967, the aircraft was accepted by the museum, after being flown from Bethpage, New York, by Grumman engineer, CAPT William E. Scarborough, USN (Ret). This was the first aircraft to be put on display in the

G-23 was rediscovered in a junk yard at Zolotian Airfield outside Managua, Nicaragua during 1961. The aircraft carried the later style Nicaraguan roundel and rudder striping. When found, the original R-1820 and Hamilton-Standard propeller were beyond repair. The new owner, J. R. Sirmons, spent four years rebuilding the aircraft to flyable condition. (J. R. Sirmons via Frank Strnad)

Naval Aviation Museum.

Today, the aircraft remains on display at the museum, now called the National Museum of Naval Aviation. While a two blade propeller was installed on the aircraft during restoration, to this day, the aircraft still mounts a Pratt & Whitney R-1340 engine. Displayed next to the aircraft is a Wright R-1820 engine which will be installed on the aircraft in the future. It is the only surviving example of the FF-1/SF-1/G-23 series in existence.

The ex-Nicaraguan G-23 was rebuilt and returned to the U.S. by Mr. Sirmons. It was later purchased by Grumman and restored to the colors and markins of VF-5B Red Rippers. The aircraft was then donated to the National Museum of Naval Aviation at Pensacola, Fl. The aircraft was one of the first to go on display at the current facility. (NAMC via Grumman)

G-23 (CC&F C/N 101) was the first Canadian Car and Foundry G-23 built and made its first flight on 3 February 1938, carrying *Fuzera Aerea de la Guardia National de Nicaragua* markings and registration (GN-3). The aircraft was overall Light Gray with all lettering in Black. The serial, GN-3 was also carried in large Black letters on the wing uppersurface. (NAMC)

Spain

In July of 1936, civil war broke out in Spain. With little indigenous capability to produce aircraft, the Spanish Nationalists and Republicans turned to other countries in search of aircraft to supply their air arms.

Ultimately receiving thirty-four examples of the G-23 during May and June of 1938, the story of how the Spanish Republican Government obtained these aircraft deserves much more space than can be spared in this text. Initially expressing interest in purchasing the G-23 legitimately during December of 1936, the Republicans were forced to obtain them illegally by forging a bogus purchase order for forty aircraft from Turkey to circumvent U.S. export laws and Canadian attitudes. In addition to the original order for forty aircraft, a subsequent order for ten additional aircraft was placed.

After assembling one aircraft for Nicaragua and one for Japan, assembly of the "Turkish" order for fifty aircraft commenced. Sixteen aircraft and eighteen fuselage assemblies were completed and shipped to St. John, New Brunswick, and eighteen wing and tail assemblies were shipped direct to St. John from the Brewster plant in New York on 2 April 1938. These aircraft were then loaded on to three freighters and shipped to Spain via Le Havre, France. One of the freighters, the HADA COUNTY, was loading the final sixteen aircraft for shipment when the illegal nature of the aircraft purchase was uncovered. The sixteen aircraft were subsequently off-loaded and temporarily stored on the dock at St John. It was these aircraft that were later sold to an extremely reluctant RCAF. Meanwhile, the thirty-four aircraft that were shipped to Le Harve were assembled, test flown and ferried to Cardedeu-Le Garriga Airfield to begin operations against the Nationalists.

The twenty-fifth G-23 built for the "Turkish" order was boxed and ready for shipment on 19 March 1938. Thirty four aircraft were shipped to Spain before government authorities became aware of their actual destination and halted further shipments. (NAMC)

A G-23 *Delfin* (AD-002) in Spanish camouflage, consisting of Dark Green and Sand upper-surfaces over Light Blue undersurfaces. The *Delfin* was capable of carrying two 110 pound bombs or twelve 22 pound bombs. With its 895 hp engine and lighter structure, its performance was superior to standard Navy FF-1s. (R. S. Allen)

The thirty-four G-23s, christened **Delfins,** by the .Republicans were assigned to **Grupo Num 28** of the Spanish Republican Air Arm, consisting of two squadrons, **la Escuadrilla** and **2a Escuadrilla**. The primary mission of the **Delfins** was to be ground attack, which resulted in the prefix 'AD' being carried on the aircraft (AD-001 -AD-034) which stood for **Asalto Delfin**.

The first combat use of the Grumman biplane did not go very well. Two **Delfins** were captured intact by the Nationalists when the pilots became disoriented and landed in Nationalist-held territory. Prior to initiation of the Republican Ebro River Offensive of 25 July 1938, the **Grupo** was split with **la Escuadrilla** remaining at Cardedeu-Le Carriga while nine aircraft of **2a Escuadrilla** were sent to Requena, Valencia for coastal patrol duty. A three aircraft detachment of **2a Escuadrilla** was also sent to the El Carmoli airfield near Cartagena for the defense of that city. During early August, the nine aircraft at Requena were redeployed to the Estremadura region of Western Spain to support Republican ground forces. Two of these aircraft were shot down on 1 September 1938 by Fiat CR. 32s of Nationalist **2-G-3 Grupo**.

The following months saw the Spanish Republicans continue to lose ground. The Catalonia region of northeastern Spain fell to the Nationalist forces in January and early February of 1939. During this time eight of the remaining **Delfins** still on strength with **la Escuidrilla** were lost, one in an accident, one was shot down, two were destroyed on the ground and four were captured by the Nationalists. March saw the collapse of Republican forces in the Estramadura region and the withdrawal of **2a Escuadrilla** back to Cartagena. It was during this time that a **Delfin** scored the only air-to-air kill by a Grumman biplane fighter, shooting down a Legion Condor Heinkel He 59B floatplane. The highlight of **Delfin** operations came on 22 March 1939, when five **Delfins** and twenty I-15s attacked an Italian troop ship attempting to enter Cartagena Harbor, inflicting high casualties. Eight days later, on 30 March, the Republicans surrendered, ending the war. That same day, the five **Delfins** flew to Oran, French Algeria seeking asylum.

Of the thirty-four G-23s shipped to Spain, twenty-three were destroyed, three being shot

This G-23 (AD-034) of *Grupo Num 28* was one of three destroyed by Spanish Nationalist forces at Villajuiga airfield on 6 February 1939. The rudder markings were (top to bottom) Red, Yellow, Purple, with the number in White. The engine cowling was Black. (Dave Lucabaugh)

down, and the rest in accidents or to anti-aircraft fire, six were captured by the Nationalists and five escaped to French Algiera. Following hostilities, the five aircraft in French Algeria were returned to Spain, and in addition to the six captured by the Nationalists during the war, were taken on strength by the *Ejercito del Aire* and assigned to *Grupo 5W*. These aircraft were then redesignated as R.6s and sent to Tetuan, Spanish Morocco where they remained

During one of their first actions, the pilots of two G-23s became disoriented and landed on Nationalist held airfields. This aircraft, AD-001, was captured intact and taken on charge by the Nationalist Air Force. The aircraft in the background is a Fiat CR 32 fighter. (R. S. Allen)

The *Delfin* was configured with underwing bomb racks for the ground attack role. One G-23 did score an air-to-air kill, shooting down a Heinkel He 59 floatplane during early 1939. (Doug Champlin)

until the last one was scrapped during 1955.

One of the last airworthy G-23s (redesignated as R-6-2) at Tutuan, Morocco during the early 1950s. The aircraft was overall Gray with Black lettering. The Spanish roundel was Red/Yellow/Red. (Grumman)

A Royal Canadian Air Force G-23 Goblin on the snow covered field at Rockcliffe, Ontario, Canada during 1940. The aircraft was camouflaged in Dark Earth and Dark Green upper-surfaces over Silver undersurfaces. The port wing undersurfaces was in Black, while the starboard wing undersurfaces was Silver. The aircraft number was carried on the underside of both lower wings. (Grumman)

Mexico

A single G-23 (CC&F construction number 148) was supplied to the Mexican government in hopes that Mexico would produce the aircraft under license. One of the sixteen airframes originally intended for the Spanish Republican Air Arm, it was flown to Mexico in September of 1939. No G-23s were ever produced in Mexico, and the fate of G-23 (CC&F cn 148) remains unknown.

Canada

Of the original forged "Turkish" order for fifty aircraft, thirty-four were delivered in April and May of 1938 before the U.S. and Canadian governments realized that the were actually bound for the Spanish Republicans. The final sixteen aircraft were already loaded aboard the freighter HADA COUNTY at St. John, New Brunswick when the Spanish plot was uncovered. With the final shipment declared illegal, the sixteen airframes were disembarked from HADA COUNTY and temporarily stored on the dock at St. John. The sixteen airframes were eventually returned to the CC&F Fort William plant.

Unable to deliver the sixteen aircraft CC&F immediately attempted to sell the aircraft to the RCAF. The RCAF on the other hand, was reluctant to buy obsolete aircraft and repeatedly avoided purchasing the aircraft. One of the sixteen G-23s (CC&F c/n 148) was sent to the

A formation of six RCAF G-23 Goblins over Nova Scotia on 16 September 1941. Three of the aircraft (341, 338 and 347) had their canopies removed after they shattered in the arctic cold of the Canadian winter. The aircraft in the foreground has a large pitot type mounted on the outboard N strut. (NAMC via R. Halford)

Mexican government in September 1939. Finally in September of 1939, with Europe at war, and the RCAF facing a critical fighter aircraft shortage, the RCAF reluctantly decided to purchase the aircraft. Delays in delivery and the hope that something better might come along delayed delivery to the RCAF until October of 1940.

Now that the RCAF had the G-23s (christened 'Goblin' by the RCAF) it did not want, the service had to decide on a suitable mission for its new aircraft. In December of 1940, the fifteen G-23s were delivered to No 118 Fighter Squadron based at Rockcliffe, Onterio. Poor serviceability and constant mechanical problems grounded the entire G-23 fleet on 10 January 1941. It was not until 1 May 1941, that the first G-23s reappeared in flying condition and by 15 June all fifteen were serviceable. During July, No 118 Squadron relocated to Dartmouth, Nova Scotia, to begin operational duties. The aircraft flew through the Summer and Fall of 1941, and, on 5 November, No 118 Squadron took delivery of its first P-40E Kittyhawk, the aircraft destined to replace the Goblin. Finally, on 12 December 1941, the Kittyhawks were placed on operational readiness, and the Goblins were officially stood down. Seven went into storage at Scoudouc, New Brunswick, and the remaining five aircraft were sent back to Rockcliffe to stand up No 123 Army Co-Operation Training Squadron (No 118 Squadron was redesignated as No 123 Squadron on 14 January 1942.) The squadron's five flyable aircraft were withdrawn from service following an incident where a pilot was nearly overcome by carbon monoxide, thus ending the Goblin's career with the RCAF. The twelve airframes were finally discarded in April of 1942, with the engines going to Army Technical Training Schools. The RCAF, and No 118 Squadron in particular, couldn't have been happier.

XSF-2

The thirty-fourth and final aircraft of the SF-1 production run (BuNo 9493) was modified to accept a 650 hp fourteen cylinder Pratt & Whitney R-1535-72 Twin Wasp Jr. air-cooled radial in place of the standard 750 hp Wright R-1820-78 radial. The aircraft was fitted with a new cowling which was similar to that used on the F2F-1 fighter and delivered under the designation XSF-2.

Armament consisted of two .30 caliber machine guns, one on a swivel mount in the rear cockpit and the other mounted in the starboard forward fuselage firing through the propeller arc. First flown on 26 November 1934, the prototype had a top speed of 202 mph. The aircraft was delivered to NAS Anacostia on 3 December and during its testing at Anacostia, the aircraft was modified with a streamlined fairing and rearward sliding canopy over the rear cockpit. The aircraft remained a single prototype, with no production order being placed.

The XSF-2 was involved in two mishaps while stationed at NAS Anacostia, one in April of 1939 and another in December of 1940. Following the last mishap, the XSF-2 was withdrawn from service and used as a ground instructional airframe at the U. S. Navy Machinist's Mate School.

The XSF-2 was modified at NAS Anacostia with a revised rear cockpit area with a rearward sliding canopy and faired in rear decking. The aircraft also had the tail hook and armament removed, with the fuselage gun port faired over. (W. L Swisher)

The XSF-2 on a test flight with everything down on 14 March 1935. The dark port on the cowling is the gun port for the forward firing .30 caliber machine gun. The aircraft was powered by a 650 hp Pratt & Whitney R-1535-72 engine. (Grumman)

Fuselage Development

SF-1

750 hp
Wright
R-1820-
78 Radial

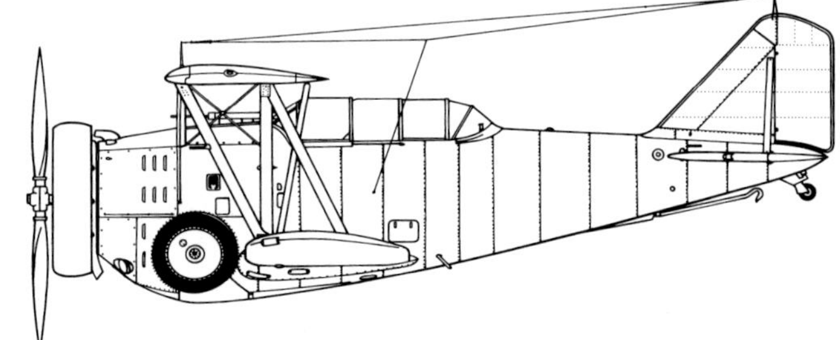

XSF-2

650 hp
Pratt &
Whitney
R-1535-
72 Radial

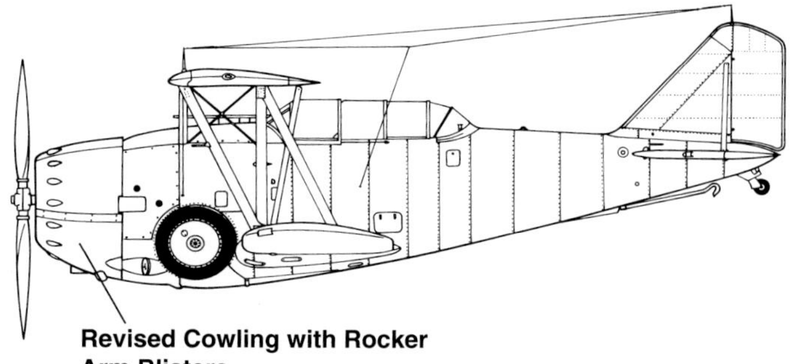

Revised Cowling with Rocker Arm Blisters

XSBF-1

In response to a U.S. Navy Bureau of Aeronautics (BuAer) design competition for a new scout bomber in late 1934 and early 1935, Grumman built a single prototype under the designation XSBF-1 (BuNo 9996). Powered by a 650 hp Pratt & Whitney R-1535-72 Twin Wasp Jr. engine, the XSBF-1 had a top speed of 215 mph. The cowling arrangement was similar to that on the XSF-2, but lacked the individual rocker arm blisters.

Armament consisted of one swivel mounted .30 caliber gun in the rear cockpit and one forward firing .30 caliber machine gun in the starboard forward fuselage. Production armament was to have consisted of two .30 caliber forward firing weapons with provisions to replace one of these with a .50 caliber gun. It was also capable of carrying one 500 pound bomb on the fuselage centerline.

Although the XSBF-1 appeared to be based on the XSF-2 airframe, there were several important differences. The nonretractable tail wheel was moved forward and the tailhook was enclosed in the fuselage similar to the F2F. Flotation bags were moved to a position just outside the interplane struts. The engine drove a variable pitch propeller and all flying surfaces were covered with fabric. Finally, the XSBF-1 was fitted with a main landing gear nearly identical to that of the XF3F-1, which offered improved landing characteristics because of its wider track.

The XSBF-1 remained on strength at at NAS Anacostia and was involved in accidents in October of 1937, September of 1938, and May of 1939. Following the last accident, the XSBF-1 was stricken from the inventory of serviceable aircraft in July of 1939.

Fuselage Development

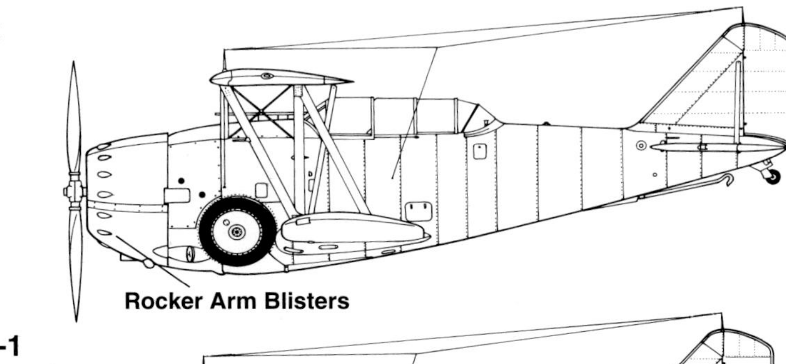

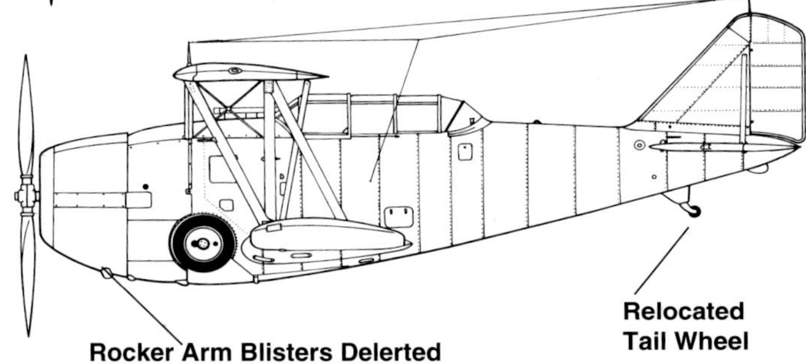

The XSBF-1 on the grass at the Grumman facility in Farmingdale, New York. The aircraft featured a landing gear configuration similar to the XF3F-1 with reduced diameter tires and used a variable pitch propeller. The carburetor air intake is visible just behind the cowling. The aircraft did not go into production. (Sid Bradd)

F2F

In the Fall of 1932, discussions between Grumman and BuAer revealed that the Navy intended to purchase a new single seat fighter to replace current fighters in the inventory, including the Grumman FF-1, which had not even gone into series production, and the Boeing F4B series.

In response to this information, Grumman submitted its design G-8, a small, single seat biplane fighter with an enclosed cockpit and retractable landing gear, similar to that used on the FF-1. Power was to be provided by a 625 hp Pratt & Whitney R-1535-44 Twin Wasp Jr. air-cooled radial engine. Estimated performance of this aircraft was expected to be much better than either the FF-1 or F4B.

Impressed with the potential of the G-8, BuAer ordered a single prototype, under the designation XF2F-1, on 2 November 1932. Later that month, Grumman moved to new facilities in Farmingdale, New York.

The construction of the XF2F-1 drew heavily on the company's prior experience with the XFF-1. The entire structure of the aircraft was aluminum. The wings and flying surfaces, however, were fabric covered. The all-metal semi-monocoque fuselage was twenty-one feet three inches long and housed a Pratt & Whitney R-1535-44 two row, fourteen cylinder, air-cooled radial engine, driving a controllable pitch two-blade Lycoming Smith propeller with a diameter of eight feet six inches. The landing gear retracted into the fuselage just forward of the lower wing. The aircraft also incorporated two innovative design features worth special mention. First, the fuselage was built with a watertight compartment placed beneath the pilot; which was used in place of flotation bags to keep the aircraft afloat in case of a forced water landing. This feature did have some success and was also used on the later F3F. Secondly, the aircraft had an adjustable horizontal stabilizer. This was used by the pilot to trim the aircraft in all flight regimes.

Construction of the XF2F-1 was completed in October of 1933, and, on 9 October, the aircraft made its first flight. It was delivered to NAS Anacostia, Virginia, on 18 October to begin BIS trials. The Board of Inspection and Survey (BIS) trails revealed that the XF2F-1

prototype had excellent performance. The aircraft had a top speed of 229 mph and a rate of climb of 3,080 feet/minute. The trials also revealed that the aircraft had poor directional stability due to it's short-coupled fuselage design. Because of this, the aircraft had a tendency to easily enter unintentional spins.

Several small changes were made to the XF2F-1 to satisfy the requests made by the Navy evaluators. As originally delivered, the XF2F-1 had a a smooth engine cowling. This was changed to a smaller diameter cowling featuring blisters over the rocker arms to allow for proper rocker arm clearance. Additionally, the oil cooler and oil cooler intake were modified, the intake changing shape from square to round. Finally, a large antenna mast was installed just forward of the vertical fin and a telescopic gun sight was installed.

With these changes, the aircraft continued the flight test program and on 17 May 1934, the Navy placed an order for fifty-four production F2F-1s. The XF2F-1 remained in service until 12 April 1938, when it was written off in an accident at NAS Anacostia.

The first production F2F-1 was delivered to the Navy on 28 January 1935. The production F2F-1 differed from the prototypes in a number of ways. The engine was replaced with a 650 hp Pratt & Whitney R-1535-72, driving a eight foot six inch Lycoming Smith controllable pitch propeller. This was later changed to a Hamilton Standard controllable pitch propeller of the same diameter. The cowling shape was modified slightly, as was the canopy. The carburetor intake was also changed and the antenna mast on the fuselage spine was deleted. Armament consisted of two .30 caliber machine guns in the fuselage, firing through the propeller arc and provision for two 110 pound bombs on underwing racks.

Production of the fifty-four aircraft on the contract (BuNos 9623-9676) was completed in August of 1935, but one additional aircraft was built (BuNo 9997). This fighter was manufactured to replace an F2F-1 (BuNo 9634); which was lost when it crashed at Woodville,

The XF2F-1 was modified with a new cowling with rocker arm blisters, a large antenna mast on the fuselage spine forward of the fin and revised oil cooler intake. The canopy also had additional bracing; which was deleted on production F2F-1s. The XF2F-1 was lost in an accident at NAS Anacostia, on 12 April 1938. (NMNA)

The XF2F-1 (BuNo 9342) on the grass field at the Grumman facility in Farmingdale on 4 October 1933. The initial prototype had a smooth cowling and square oil cooler intake. The aircraft was overall Light Gray with Aluminum doped fabric surfaces. The top of the upper wing was Chrome Yellow. (Sid Bradd)

Development

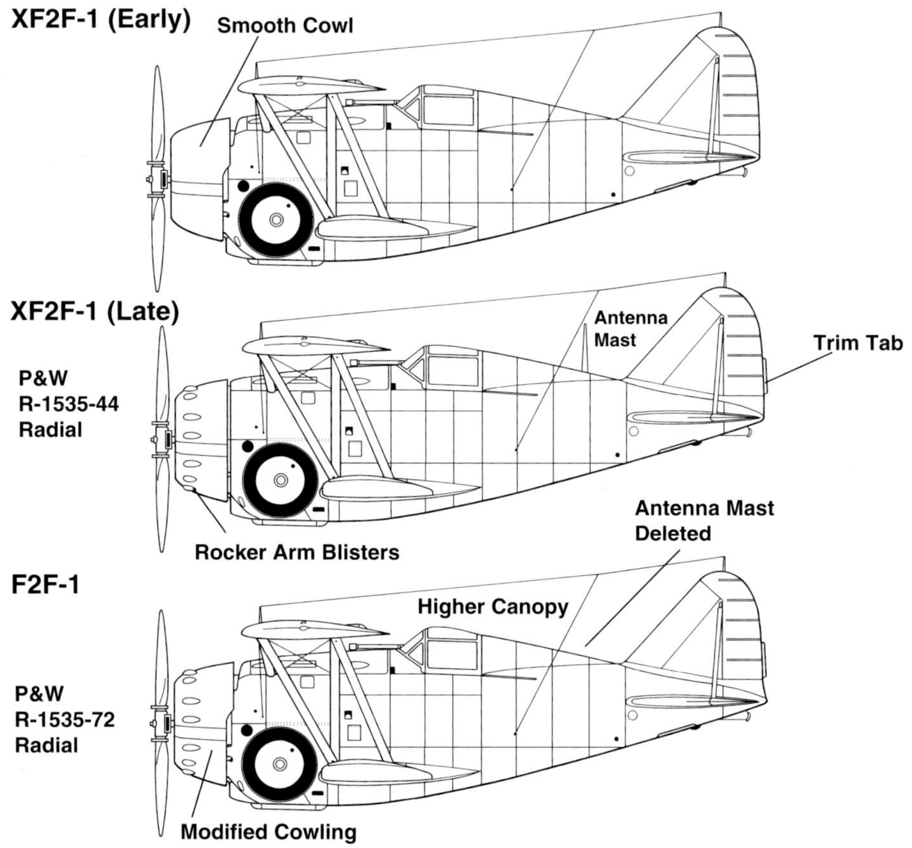

The cockpit and instrument panel of an F2F-1. The telescopic gun sight is in the center of the windscreen. The Gray object just below the instrument cluster is a retractable plotting board for navigation. The throttle quadrant is on the lower left. (Gurmman)

Mississippi on 16 March 1935, during its delivery flight to San Diego. The aircraft was intended for VF-2B.

VF-2B was the first squadron to transition to the F2F-1. VF-2B was unique in that the squadron was manned primarily with enlisted pilots (officers flew as section leaders). The "Flying Chiefs" went on to amass a record unrivaled by any other Navy fighter squadron. VF-2B (later VF-2) operated F2F-1s continuously from February of 1935 until October of 1940. In 1938 and 1939 every aircraft in VF-2 had the Battle "E" award for gunnery painted on the fuselage. This was the first time a squadron had held that honor two years in a row and was a tribute to the aggressiveness and determination of the entire squadron.

Following VF-2B, VF-3B also transitioned to the F2F-1 during 1935. The squadron operated their F2F-1s aboard USS RANGER, initially, but, during 1937, the squadron was redesignated VF-7B with orders to become part of the USS YORKTOWN air group. In July of 1937, the unit's designator was changed again, this time to VF-5, to correspond with YORKTOWN's hull number (CV-5).

Four other squadrons also operated the F2F-1, VF-5B operated nine F2F-1s alongside its FF-1s; while awaiting deliveries of F3F-1s. These same nine aircraft were loaned to VB-5B

for a short time during 1936. VF-7 took delivery of two and VF-4M (later VMF-2) operated three during 1937, while awaiting F3F-1s.

By 1940, F2Fs began to disappear from front line service. Some were assigned to Patrol Wings, while a majority were used as advanced fighter-trainers, primarily at NAS Miami and NAS Pensacola, Florida. The last F2F-1 was removed from service during 1942. Not one example of the F2F-1 survives today.

This F2F-1 (BuNo 9643) of VF-2 had a significant oil leak which spread oil back over the cowling. Engine exhaust stains cover the wheel covers making them appear Black. The aicraft has a Battle E award on the fusealge. This F2F-1 was lost at NAS Miami during October of 1941; while serving as an advanced trainer. (Sid Bradd)

"

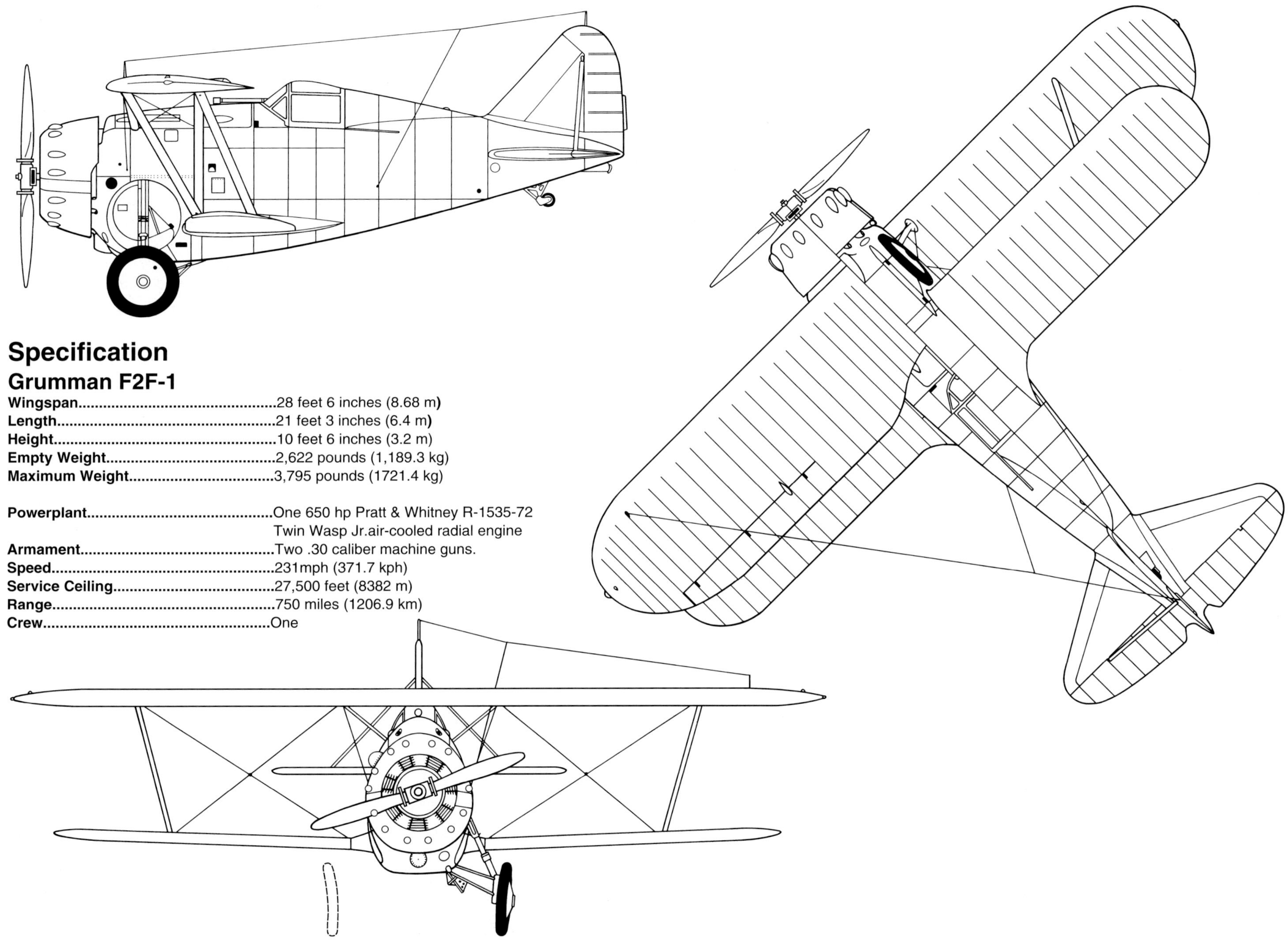

Specification

Grumman F2F-1

Wingspan..28 feet 6 inches (8.68 m)
Length..21 feet 3 inches (6.4 m)
Height..10 feet 6 inches (3.2 m)
Empty Weight..2,622 pounds (1,189.3 kg)
Maximum Weight...................................3,795 pounds (1721.4 kg)

Powerplant..One 650 hp Pratt & Whitney R-1535-72
Twin Wasp Jr.air-cooled radial engine
Armament...Two .30 caliber machine guns.
Speed..231mph (371.7 kph)
Service Ceiling......................................27,500 feet (8382 m)
Range..750 miles (1206.9 km)
Crew..One

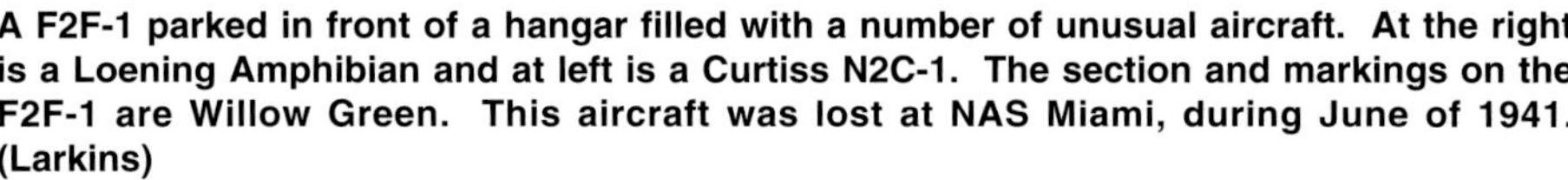

A F2F-1 parked in front of a hangar filled with a number of unusual aircraft. At the right is a Loening Amphibian and at left is a Curtiss N2C-1. The section and markings on the F2F-1 are Willow Green. This aircraft was lost at NAS Miami, during June of 1941. (Larkins)

A F2F-1 (BuNo 9671) of VF-5 was being hoisted out of the water by a crane aboard USS YORKTOWN during 1938. The watertight compartment in the fuselage kept the aircraft afloat long enough for it to be salvaged. This F2F was later lost at NAS Miami in October of 1941. (Tailhook Photo Service)

This F2F-1 (BuNo 9623) was assigned to Naval Air Station Seattle, Washington during early 1941 as a gunnery trainer for patrol aircraft. This was the first production F2F-1 and it ended its days as a trainer at NAS Miami before being lost in a crash in June of 1941. The aircraft is overall Light Gray with Black lettering. (Larkins)

A trio of F2F-1 of VF-2B fly formation during the mid-1930s. VF-2B was known as the Flying Chiefs and was manned by enlisted pilots (except for section leaders and the XO and CO). During 1938 and 1939, the squadron won back to back Battle E awards for gunnery while flying F2Fs. The aircraft in the foreground has the canopy removed. (Larkins)

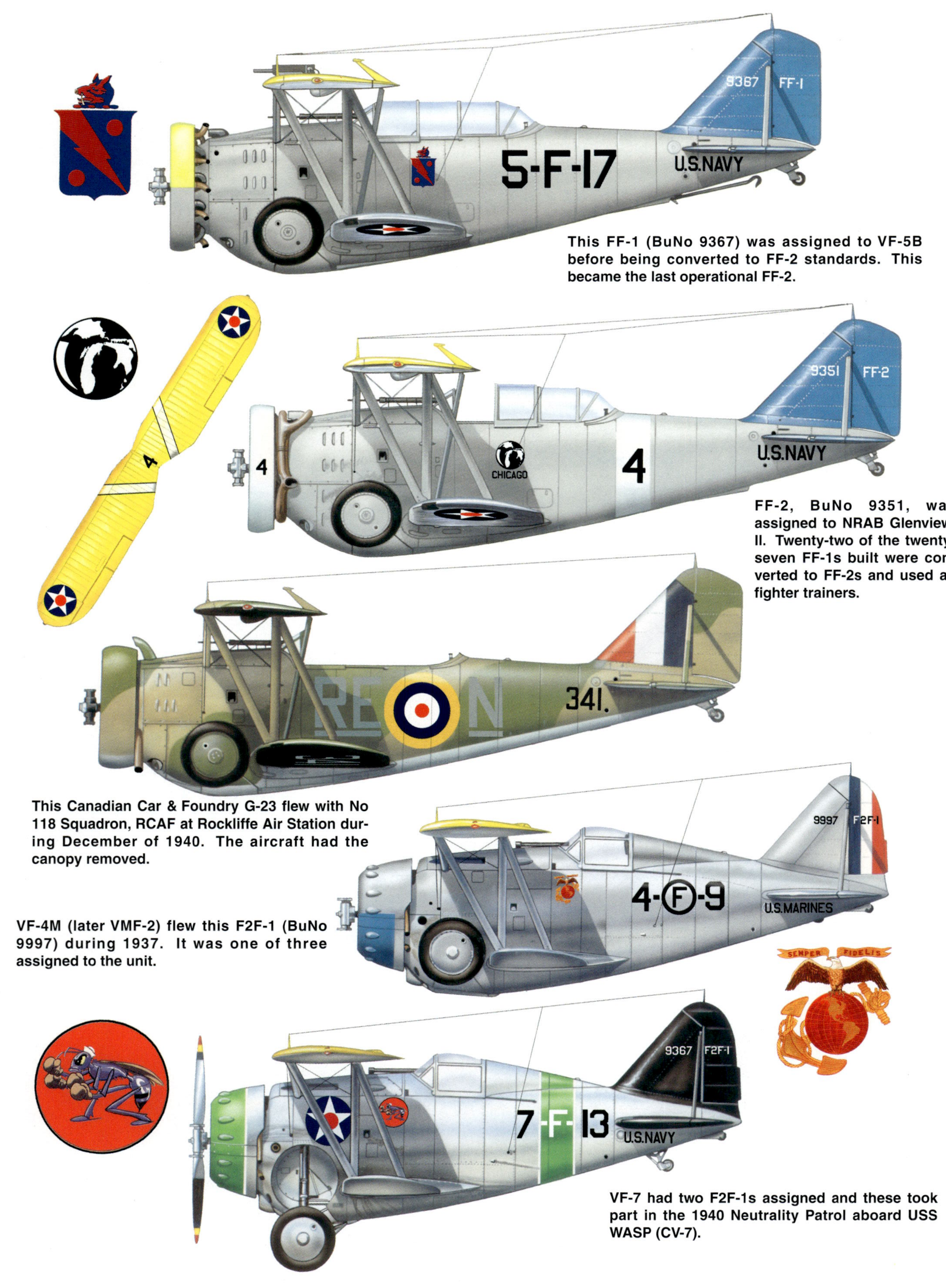

This FF-1 (BuNo 9367) was assigned to VF-5B before being converted to FF-2 standards. This became the last operational FF-2.

FF-2, BuNo 9351, was assigned to NRAB Glenview, Il. Twenty-two of the twenty-seven FF-1s built were converted to FF-2s and used as fighter trainers.

This Canadian Car & Foundry G-23 flew with No 118 Squadron, RCAF at Rockliffe Air Station during December of 1940. The aircraft had the canopy removed.

VF-4M (later VMF-2) flew this F2F-1 (BuNo 9997) during 1937. It was one of three assigned to the unit.

VF-7 had two F2F-1s assigned and these took part in the 1940 Neutrality Patrol aboard USS WASP (CV-7).

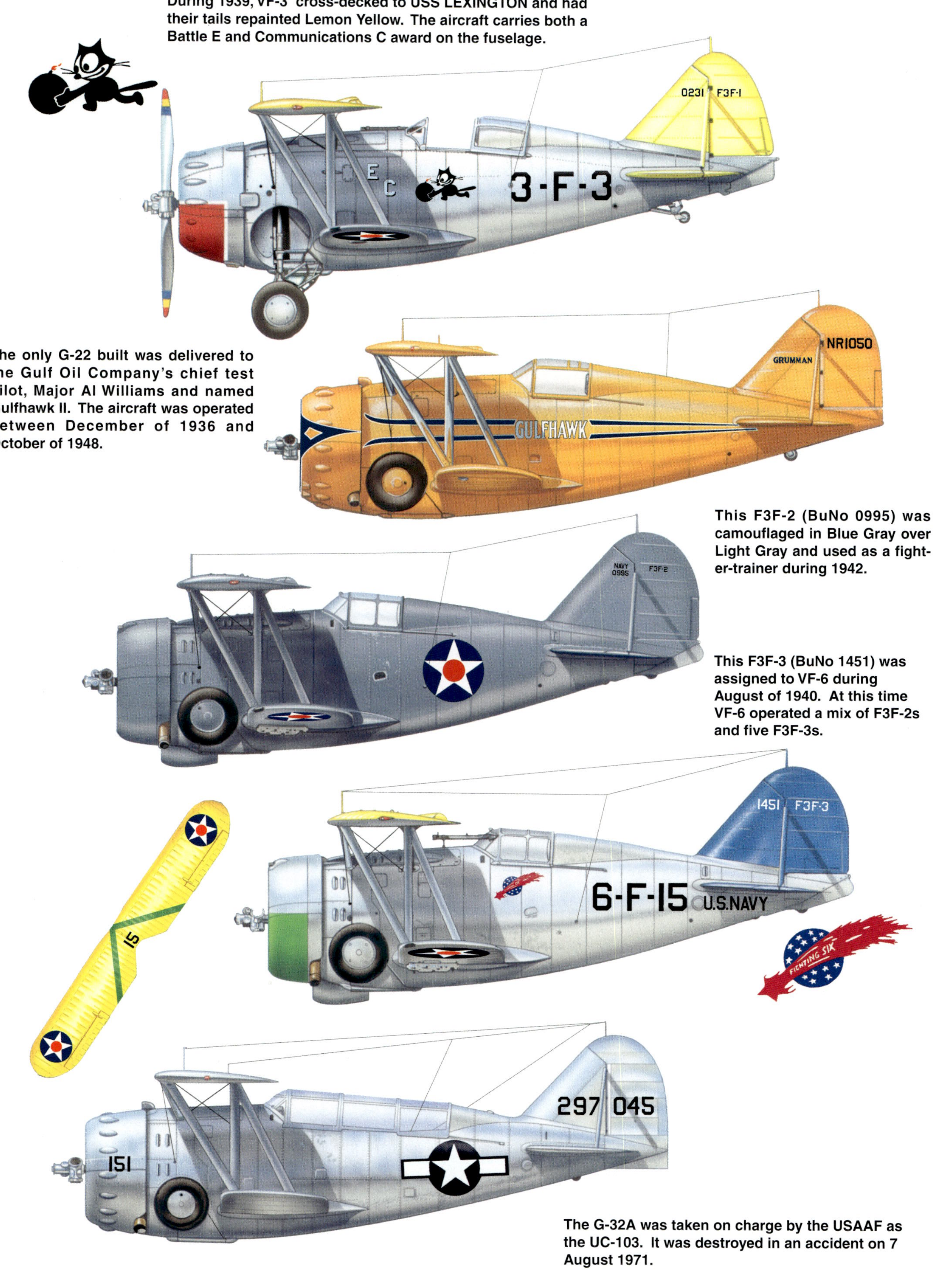

During 1939, VF-3 cross-decked to USS LEXINGTON and had their tails repainted Lemon Yellow. The aircraft carries both a Battle E and Communications C award on the fuselage.

The only G-22 built was delivered to the Gulf Oil Company's chief test pilot, Major Al Williams and named Gulfhawk II. The aircraft was operated between December of 1936 and October of 1948.

This F3F-2 (BuNo 0995) was camouflaged in Blue Gray over Light Gray and used as a fighter-trainer during 1942.

This F3F-3 (BuNo 1451) was assigned to VF-6 during August of 1940. At this time VF-6 operated a mix of F3F-2s and five F3F-3s.

The G-32A was taken on charge by the USAAF as the UC-103. It was destroyed in an accident on 7 August 1971.

F2F-1s of VF-5 aboard USS YORKTOWN (CV-5) during February of 1939. The large Black Y on the ship's island was a recognition marking used to help distinguish her from the other ships of the YORKTOWN Class. Later, the squadron transitioned to the F3F-3. (Tailhook Photo Service)

The remains of a F2F-1 that crashed near Norwood, Colorado, killing the pilot, 1st Lieutenant Glen Herndon, USMC. The aircraft carried the markings of VF-4M (later VMF-2) and was one of three F2Fs delivered to the unit. (Roger Seybel)

VF-2's second section fly in the squadron's famous "Razzle Dazzle" formation on 16 March 1940. Both wingmen are flying in out of balance flight; while the leader flies straight and level. The Flying Chiefs flew the F2F longer than any other squadron, from February 1935 to October of 1940. (W. L. Swisher)

A F2F-1 (BuNo 9663) of VMF-2. Three F2F-1s were delivered to the unit as interim equipment; while awaiting delivery of F3F-2s. 2-MF-9 had True Blue section markings, Red, White and Blue tail stripes and the Marine Corps insignia on the fuselage below the cockpit. (Larkins)

VF-2's commanding officer, Lieutenant Commander Apollo Soucek and his plane captain, Aviation Machinist Mate First Class J. Stok pose with the CO's F2F-1 at Naval Air Station North Island California during September of 1937. The unit marking consisted of a Chief Petty Officer's rating badge and the Latin inscription "Adorimini." (Tailhook Photo Service)

A F2F-1 (BuNo 9659) in flight over San Diego during 1939. VF-2 waas cross-decked to the USS SARATOGA during 1939 for her training cruise. As part of Carrier Air Group Three, the unit had the tails of their F2Fs painted White. This aircraft has Lemon Yellow section markings. (USN via W. L. Swisher)

F2F-1s of VF-7 at Parris Island, South Carolina on 3 March 1940. Fighting Seven was assigned to USS WASP (CV-7) and flew two F2Fs. The fuselage star indicates that these aircraft were involved in the 1940 Neutrality Patrol aboard USS WASP. A F3F-1 is behind 7-F-13 and the aircraft in the background is a JF-2 of VMU-1. (Larkins)

A line-up of F2F-1s of VF-5B Red Rippers on the ramp of their home station. All are equipped with gun cameras on the upper wing center section. The aircraft in the foreground is BuNo 9669. VF-5B was stationed aboard the USS RANGER (CV-4). (W. L. Swisher)

F3F-1

On 15 October 1934, with the delivery of the first production F2F-1 still three and a half months away, Grumman was awarded a contract for a single prototype of the Grumman model G-11 under the designation XF3F-1. The XF3F-1 was an attempt on the part of Grumman to rectify the shortcomings of the F2F, primarily in the areas of directional stability and stall characteristics. In addition, performance gains were expected from the new fighter.

Looking like a stretched F2F-1, the fuselage of the XF3F-1 was lengthened by some twenty-one inches over the earlier aircraft. This was done to improve longitudinal stability. The F3F-1 also had larger wings than it's predecessor, with a wingspan of thirty-two feet. The aircraft was powered by a 650 hp Pratt & Whitney R-1535-72 air-cooled radial engine driving a eight foot six inch Lycoming Smith two blade, controllable pitch propeller. The armament of the prototype was two .30 caliber machine guns firing through the propeller and provision for two 100 pound bombs on underwing bomb racks. The F2F-1 had 30x5 tires and the XF3F-1 used 26x6 tires. The carburetor air intake was moved from the starboard side of the forward fuselage to a position on the port side just above the landing gear well .

The prototype XF3F-1 (BuNo 9727) flew for the first time on 20 March 1935, with Grumman test pilot Jimmy Collins at the controls. Two days later the aircraft was totally destroyed when Collins overstressed the aircraft during a dive demonstration. Pulling well over 9Gs, the aircraft disintegrated at 8,000 feet, shedding the engine and wings. The remaining structure crashed about two miles east of the Farmingdale plant, killing Collins. As witnesses attempted to remove the pilot from the aircraft, the wreckage caught fire. The G forces experienced during the pullout were enough to cause the bomb rack bolts to fail.

Construction began on a second XF3F-1 prototype immediately. This aircraft was assigned the same Bureau Number as the first prototype (BuNo 9727). Incorporating minor modifications, the second XF3F-1 was externally identical to the first aircraft. The first flight of the second prototype occurred on 9 May 1935. Four days later, the aircraft was flown to NAS Anacostia to resume service acceptance trials. On 17 May 1935, while the aircraft was conducting spin tests at the Naval Proving Ground in Dahlgren, Virginia, the second prototype crashed. The pilot, Lee Gehlbach, was unable to recover from a right-hand spin, and bailed out at 2,000 feet. After fifty-two turns in the spin, the XF3F-1 impacted a wooded area, destroying the wings and forward fuselage.

Following the second crash, a third XF3F-1 was built, flying for the first time on 7 June 1935. Undamaged parts from the second prototype were used in the construction of the third aircraft. This prototype differed from the others, incorporating a larger rudder to improve spin recovery characteristics. Additionally, two hinged panels were installed under the fuselage to the rear of the tailhook opening. These modifications delayed commencement of BIS trials until 10 July.

While not installed on the third prototype, it was determined that production aircraft would use the Pratt & Whitney R-1535-84 engine in place of the R-1535 -72. Production aircraft would also use a Hamilton Standard eight foot six inch controllable pitch propeller in place of the Lycoming Smith propeller. To simulate the additional 43.4 pounds of weight that these modifications would add to the aircraft, a fifteen inch circular steel tube filled with lead was bolted to the front of the engine crankcase.

Flight testing of the XF3F-1 was given priority and by 1 August, BuAer accepted the XF3F-1 for service. On 24 August 1935, the Navy ordered fifty-four production aircraft under the designation F3F-1s (BuNos 0211-0264). The XF3F-1 continued flight testing until March of 1936, when it was transferred to NAS Anacostia as a station aircraft. The XF3F-1 ended it's days as an advanced fighter-trainer at NAS Miami during 1943.

Deliveries of production F3F-1s began in January of 1936 and the last aircraft was delivered in September of the same year. Production aircraft differed very little from the third prototype. F3F-1s were fitted with the 650 hp Pratt & Whitney R-1535-84 engine (700 hp for take-off). Additionally, the starboard .30 caliber machine gun was replaced by .50 caliber gun. This was to become the standard armament of the F3F series. Finally, a eight foot six inch Hamilton Standard propeller was used in place of the Lycoming Smith unit. As with the FF-1 and F2F, the F3F-1 had an adjustable horizontal stabilizer with a movement range of +3.75 to -2.5 degrees.

VF-5B was the first squadron to transition to the F3F-1, followed by VF-6B. In January of 1937, Marine Corps squadron VF-4M took delivery of the first of six F3F-1s while awaiting deliveries of F3F-2s.

On 1 July 1937, naval aviation underwent a sweeping reorganization. All squadrons in an air group were given the same number as the carrier that they were assigned to, for example:

Pre 7/1/37 CV/Tail Color		Post 7/1/37 CV/ Tail Color	
VF-2B	LEX/Yellow	VF-2	LEX (CV-2)/Yellow
VF-3B	RNGR/Green	VF-5	YKTN (CV-5)/Red
VF-5B	RNGR/Blue	VF-4	RNGR (CV-4)/Green
VF-6B	SARA/White	VF-3	SARA (CV-3)/ White
VF-4M	FMF S.D./RWB	VMF-2	FMF S.D./RWB Stripes
		VF-6	ENT (CV-6)/Blue
		VF-7	WASP (CV-7)/Black

The Grumman XF3F-1 prototype on the grass field at the Grumman Farmingdale, New York plant on 20 March 1935. This was the first of three XF3F-1 prototypes. This aircraft was destroyed two days later when the test pilot, Jimmy Collins, overstressed the aircraft in a dive. The aircraft disintegrated, killing Collins. The first XF3F-1 used the same rudder as the F2F-1 series. (Grumman)

During the Summer of 1936, all F3F-1s were restricted to 6G, following several accidents. Following these mishaps, F3F-1 (BuNo 0213) was flown to the Naval Aircraft Factory for static testing. As a result of this testing, the upper wing beam and aileron bell cranks were strengthened on all subsequent F3Fs and retrofitted to F3F-1s.

One additional squadron received F3F-1s. With the commissioning of USS WASP [CV-7], Fighting Seven (VF-7) was commissioned. In December of 1939, VF-7 received half of VF-3s F3F-1s when that squadron transitioned to the Brewster F2A-1 Buffalo. Eventually, VF-7 would operate fifteen F3F-1s and two F2F-1s.

As newer aircraft reached the fleet, F3F-1s were gradually withdrawn from combat squadrons and sent to the Training Command. The last F3F-1s were turned in on 10 February 1941 as VF-71 and VF-72 (formerly VB-7 and VF-7) began to receive F4F-3s. A majority of F3F-1s went to NAS Miami and NAS Norfolk. What aircraft student aviators didn't destroy were sent to Technical Training Schools as newer types came to the Training Command.

Development

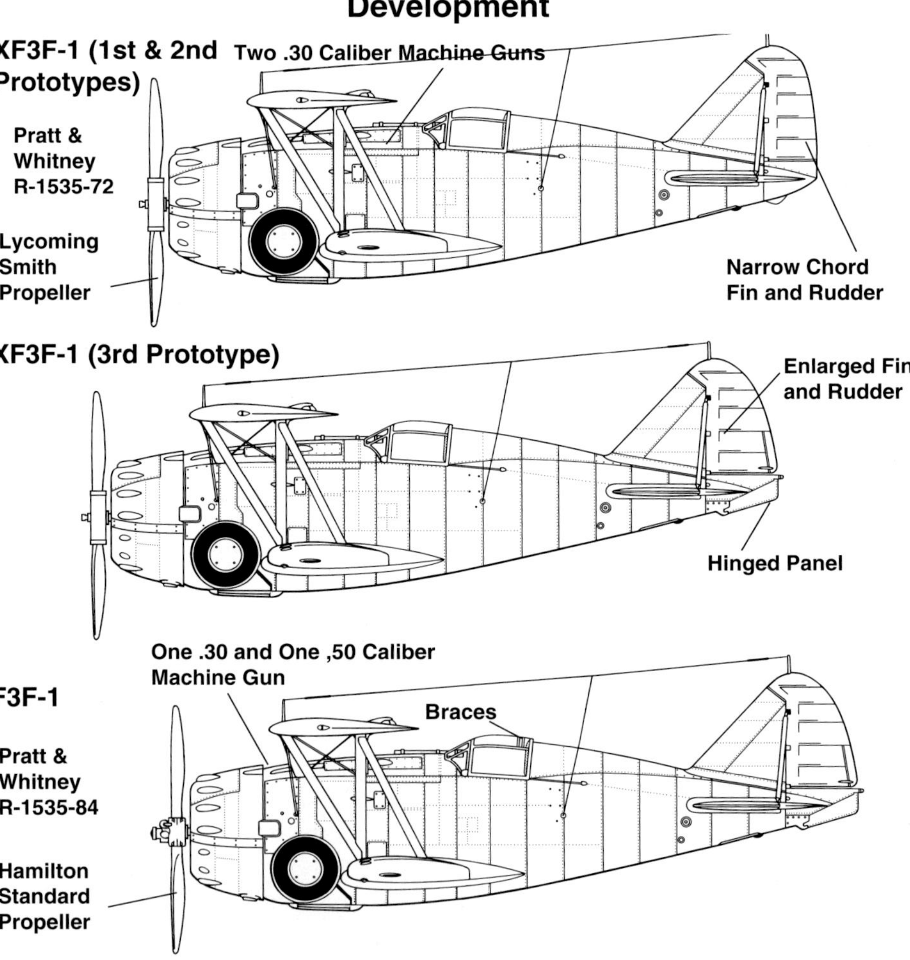

XF3F-1 (BuNo 9727), the second prototype, was lost on 17 May 1935, when the pilot, Lee Gehlbach, was unable to recover from a spin and bailed out. Parts from this aircraft were used to built the third prototype. (Grumman)

The third F3F-1 prototype had the same BuNo as the second prototype. The aircraft had a larger rudder and hinged panels on the lower fuselage to improve its spin recovery characteristics. The aircraft had a 43.4 pound weight attached to the engine crankcase to simulate the weight of the R-1535-84 engine and Hamilton Standard propeller intended for production aircraft. (Larkins)

A F3F-1 (BuNo 0221) on the grass as NAS Anacostia on 12 April 1936, during acceptance trails. The aircraft was delivered to VF-5B the next day. It was lost at sea after striking the mast of a destroyer during a landing attempt, killing the pilot. The tails surfaces were True Blue and the section markings were Black. (Dave Lucabaugh)

In the fleet reorganization of 1 July 1937, VF-5B became VF-4 with the tail surfaces changing color from True Blue to Willow Green. The parent carrier remained USS RANGER (CV-4). This F3F last served as a fighter-trainer at NAS Miami before being lost in a crash during February of 1941. (Doug Olson)

The commissioning of USS WASP (CV-7) led to the requirement for an additional fighter squadron in her air group. Fighting Seven (VF-7) was formed and equipped with F3F-1s. This F3F-1 (BuNo 0239) on the field at Hampton Roads, Virginia on 15 April 1940 was equipped with a Mk XLIII training bomb rack under the starboard wing and carried the Neutrality Star on the nose. (W. L. Swisher)

While VF-2 was temporarily assigned to USS SARATOGA, VF-3 was temporarily assigned to USS LEXINGTON. For this reason, the tails of VF-3 aircraft were painted Lemon Yellow. This F3F-1 (BuNo 0231) carried a Battle E on the fuselage as well as a C award for communications proficiency. The aircraft in the background has a F3F-2 style canopy and may be the XF3F-2; which was placed into fleet service as a F3F-1. (CAPT Lewis M.D. Ford via D. Bruce VanAlstine)

When U.S. Naval Aviation reorganized on 1 July 1937, VF-4M became known as VMF-2. F3F-1 (BuNo 0256) was assigned to the second section leader and had White section markings and the Marine Corps Globe and Anchor insignia on the fuselage under the cockpit. VMF-2 soon converted from the F3F-1 to the F3F-2. (Larkins)

While awaiting deliveries of the F3F-2, VF-4M took delivery of six F3F-1s. This F3F-1 (BuNo 0251), on the ramp at NAS North Island, California, was assigned to the commanding officer. It was later written off in a crash in August of 1937. (W. L. Swisher)

This F3F-1 (BuNo 0239) was initially assigned to Fighting Six (VF-6B) and had White tail surfaces and Black section markings. It later served with VF-7 and ended its career at Naval Technical Training School Memphis, Tenn. The Felix the Cat emblem is still in use today by VF-31, based at NAS Miramar, California, flying Grumman F-14D Tomcats. (Campbell Archives/OKC)

Fighting Six (VF-6B) became Fighting Three (VF-3) under the fleet reorganization of July 1937. The tail color did not change, nor did the parent carrier, USS SARATOGA (CV-3). This F3F-1 was visiting the Griffith Park National Guard Airfield in Los Angeles, California and had White tail surfaces and Lemon Yellow section markings. The name stenciled on the canopy frame was "Cadet Cooper." The aircraft was equipped with a Mk III gun camera mounted on the upper wing center section. (W. L. Swisher)

F3F-1 of VF-4 line the bow of USS RANGER (CV-4) as she steams in formation with USS LEXINGTON (CV-2) and USS SARATOGA (CV-3). The seven aircraft on the bow are Vought SBU-1 scout bombers of Scouting Forty-two (VS-42) with rear facing wing chevrons. (Tailhook Photo Service)

A F3F-1 (BuNo 0235) launches from USS RANGER (CV-4) on 28 March 1938. The side number was 4-F-13 and it had Willow Green section markings. The pilot has the rudder hard over to counteract the engine torque. (Dave Lucabaugh)

This F3F-1 crashed near NAS Miami, Fl on 27 May 1942. The aircraft was carrying a Mk XLIII bomb carrier and had the tail surfaces in Insignia Red with the fuselage numbers in Black. The aircraft had previously served with NAS Anacostia, VF-4, VF-3 and VF-71. (Tailhook Photo Service)

Mk III Gun Camera Installation

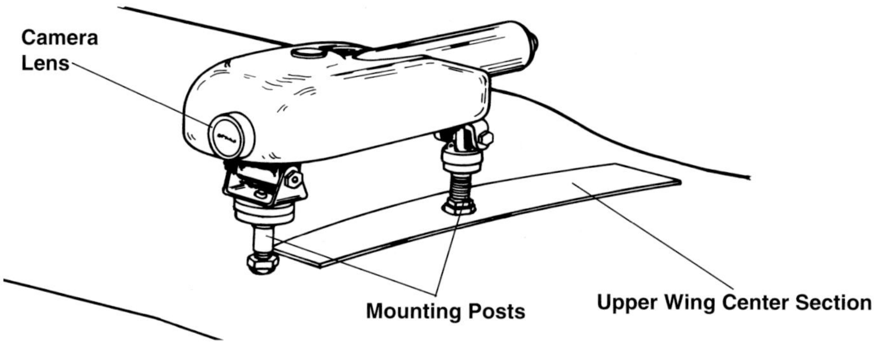

F3F-2

In November, 1935, the U.S. Navy Bureau of Aeronautics initiated a request for proposals for a single seat carrier fighter to replace the F2Fs and F3F-1s, the latter which was just about to enter service. In response, Grumman submitted Design 16, designated the XF4F-1, a biplane similar in appearance to the F3F series. Grumman was awarded a contract for the development of the XF4F-1 on 2 March 1936, and, three months later, Brewster was awarded a contract for one prototype of Brewster Design B-139, a monoplane, under the designation XF2A-1.

Concurrent with the development of the XF4F-1, separate Grumman studies indicated that the performance of the F3F airframe fitted with a 865 hp Wright R-182O-G5 Cyclone would be nearly identical to that of the proposed XF4F-1. With it's status as the premier supplier of carrier fighter aircraft threatened by the XF2A-1 monoplane, Grumman requested that the contract for the XF4F-1 biplane be modified, proposing the development of the G-18 monoplane in it's place, under the designation of XF4F-2, the initial prototype of the Wildcat series. On 10 June 1936, BuAer approved the amended contract.

One week prior to this, on 3 June 1936, Grumman requested a modification to the F3F-1 production contract, asking permission to modify the fifty-fourth and final F3F-1 to accept a 865 hp Wright R-1820-G5 Cyclone two-speed supercharged air-cooled radial engine. Work on the necessary modifications began and a contract for the XF3F-2 was signed 28 July 1936. Interestingly, the prototype was delivered to NAS Anacostia the day before the contract was signed. The first flight occurred on 21 July 1936.

The Cyclone installation required a redesign of the forward fuselage of the F3F-1 airframe to accept the larger diameter of the Wright engine. The XF3F-2 (BuNo 0451) also replaced the two blade Hamilton Standard propeller with a three blade nine foot eight inch diameter Hamilton Standard. Even with the increased forward area, the higher power of the Wright engine, coupled with the two speed supercharger and three blade propeller, gave the XF3F-2 a maximum speed of 255 mph. Supercharging also increased the service ceiling of the aircraft to 30,200 feet.

In spite of the early delivery of the aircraft, service trials did not begin until January of 1937. Problems with carburetion, oil cooling and carbon monoxide in the cockpit stalled the trials. The prototype had the oil cooler inside the lower lip of the engine cowling and this proved to be inadequate. The carbon monoxide in the cockpit was caused by poor airflow within the fuselage. Flight testing resumed in January of 1937 and on 23 March 1937, BuAer signed a contract for eighty-one production aircraft under the designation F3F-2.

When the first production F3F 2 (BuNo 0967) was delivered to NAS Anacostia on 27 July, it incorporated a new rudder shape with increased area to compensate for the increased engine torque of the higher powered engine. A new canopy and windshield were installed, but carbon monoxide problems remained. Oil cooling problems also remained. Because of this, fleet introduction was delayed until 4 November 1937. When the second F3F-2 (BuNo 0968) was accepted by the Navy, it incorporated the necessary modifications needed to remedy these problems. A larger oil cooler was installed in a fairing placed below the fuselage between the main landing gear. The cockpit carbon monoxide problem was completely eliminated by placing fair inlets just above the leading edge of the horizontal stabilizers. Finally, with all major problems fixed, production aircraft started rolling off the assembly line. One further modification to production

The XF3F-2 (BuNo 0452) suspended at Grumman's Farmingdale facility just prior to its first flight. The installation of the Wright Cyclone engine altered the nose section, but little else differed from the F3F-1. Mechanical problems and a move to Bethpage, Long Island, New York, delayed fleet introduction until 4 November 1937. (Grumman)

aircraft was the addition of accessory air cooling vents on the four inspection panels on the fuselage immediately behind the engine cowling.

On 29 November 1937, F3F-2 (BuNo 0968) was delivered to VF-6 as the Commanding Officer's aircraft, initiating fleet usage of the type. F3F-2 (BuNo 0969) was also delivered to VF-6. After these two aircraft, VMF 2 and VF-6 each received there full compliment of aircraft.

The first production F3F-2 (BuNo 0967) on the Bethpage ramp. This aircraft lacked the oil cooler fairing under the nose and fresh air inlets on the fuselage for proper ventilation. The aircraft was armed with two 110 pound bombs on its underwing bomb racks. The bulge within the underwing star is a landing light. (Grumman)

This F3F-2 (BuNo 0998) was assigned to the fifth section leader of Fighting Six (VF-6). The aircraft had Willow Green section markings outlined in Black. The aircraft also carried a Battle E award on the fuselage and a White Winged Turtle marking on the fin. The winged turtle indicated that this F3F-2 had flown across the equator. (Larkins)

craft. With VMF-2 and VF-6 both fully equipped, VMF-,1 based at MCAS Quantico, Virginia, became the final squadron to transition to the type. Additionally, VF-5 operated four F3F-2s, but was primarily equipped with F3F-3s.

The production F3F-2 was powered by a Wright R-1820-22 Cyclone engine rated at 950 hp for takeoff. Maximum speed was 256 mph and service ceiling was 32,400 feet. Fuel capacity was increased from the F3F-1 to 130 gallons; which gave the aircraft a range of 825 miles. Armament consisted of one .50 caliber and one .30 caliber machine gun mounted in the nose firing through the propeller arc. Additionally, two 110 pound bombs could be carried on under wing Mk XLI bomb racks.

As Brewster F2A-2s and Grumman F4F-3s started reaching the fleet in October of 1940, biplanes began to disappear from front line service. VF-6 turned in their F3F-2s for F4F-3s in early1941. Finally, on 10 October 1941, VMF-2 turned in their F3F-2s, becoming the last naval aviation fighter squadron to operate biplanes.

Once removed from fleet service, F3F-2s were assigned to the Training Command at various bases including NAS Miami, Florida and NAS Corpus Christi, Texas. It was an F3F-2 that was the last of the F3F series to be removed from service. In November of 1943, F3F-2 (BuNo 0983) was retired, thus ending the flying days of all F3F aircraft.

Two aircraft, based on the F3F-2, were proposed but never built. The G-24 was to be an advanced trainer while the G-37 was to be an export model.

No F3F-2s survived the Second World War, however, in April of 1990, a F3F-2 (BuNo 0976) was discovered in 1,800 feet of water about ten miles off the coast of Del Mar, California. On 29 August 1940, Marine 1st Lieutenant Robert E. Galer had ditched this aircraft following a fuel pump failure. Lieutenant Galer later went on to earn the Medal of Honor as the commanding officer of VMF-224 flying F4F-3/4 Wildcats on Guadalcanal during 1943. Restoration of the aircraft was completed in February of 1994.

While no completely original F3F-2s remain in flyable condition, three essentially "new build" F3F-2s were flown in early 1993. Built by the Texas Aircraft Factory of Fort Worth,

Development

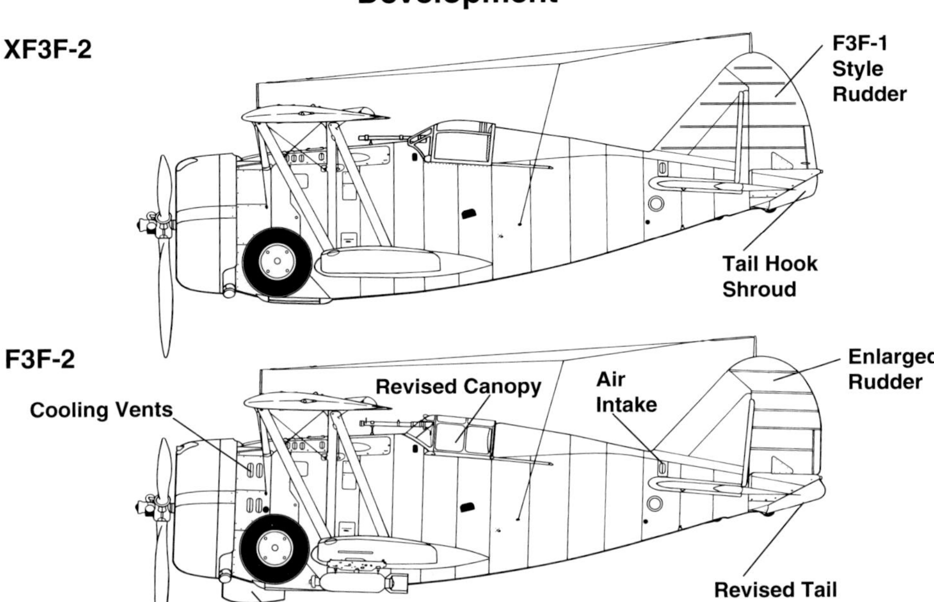

Texas, one was delivered to the Lone Star Flight Museum of Galvaston, Texas, and the other two went to Cinema Air, Inc. of Palomar, California. While incorporating some original parts, these aircraft were essentially manufactured to Grumman specifications, except for new avionics, wheel brakes and 1,050 hp R-1820-50 engines. These aircraft differ little externally from production F3Fs, and are drawing tremendous interest everywhere they go.

A F3F-2 (BuNo 0969) at Floyd Bennett Field, New York. The aircraft was equipped with Mk XLI bomb racks and the larger diameter of the .50 caliber machine is readily visible. The aircraft had Insignia Red section markings and a True Blue tail. It was lost in April of 1941, while attached to NAS Pearl Harbor. (Warren Shipp)

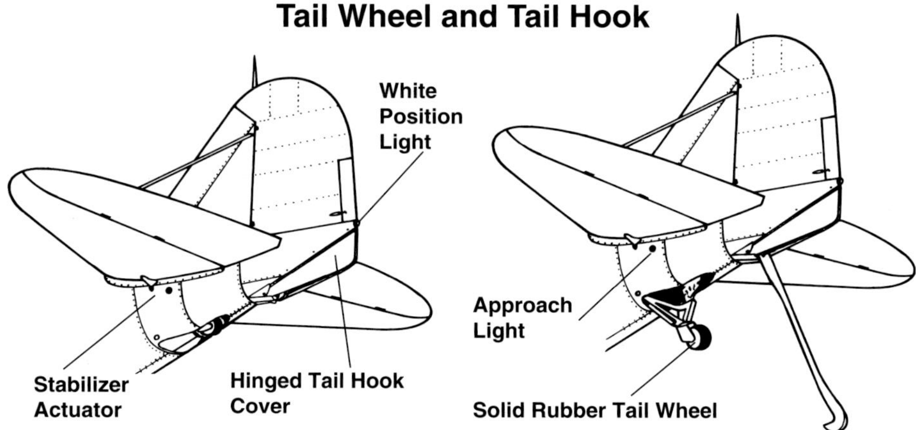

F3F-2s aboard USS ENTERPRISE (CV-6). All of the aircraft have canvas covers over the canopy, guns and engines. These covers are normally stored in a compartment behind the cockpit. The aircraft at the left (6-F-20) was one of two spares on strength with VF-6 during 1938. (NMNA)

(Left) This F3F-2 (BuNo 9972) of VMF-2 engages the barrier after the tail hook failed aboard USS SARATOGA on 8 October 1940. The oil cooler fairing is missing from the aircraft. (Dave Lucabaugh)

A F3F-2 (BuNo 0994) of VMF-2 on the ramp of the Griffith Park National Guard Airfield on 1 May 1938. Section markings are Willow Green and the rudder stripes are Red/White/Blue. The unit insignia on the fin was a Red and Black leaping Lion in a Green circle bordered in Red. This F3F was lost in a crash at NAS Corpus Christi, Texas on 9 July 1942. (W. L. Swisher)

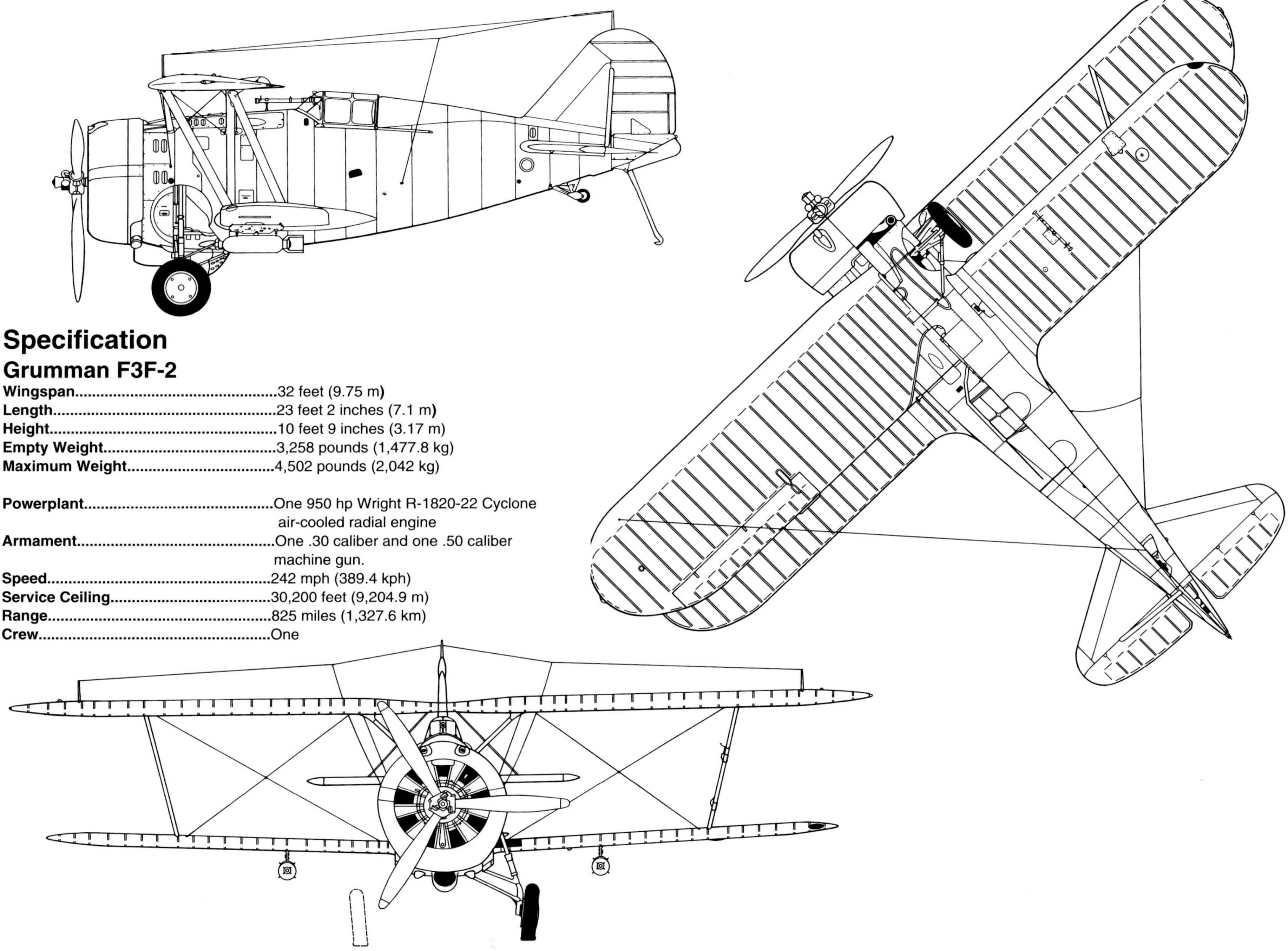

Specification

Grumman F3F-2

Wingspan..32 feet (9.75 m**)**
Length..23 feet 2 inches (7.1 m**)**
Height..10 feet 9 inches (3.17 m)
Empty Weight...3,258 pounds (1,477.8 kg)
Maximum Weight......................................4,502 pounds (2,042 kg)

Powerplant..One 950 hp Wright R-1820-22 Cyclone
air-cooled radial engine
Armament..One .30 caliber and one .50 caliber
machine gun.
Speed..242 mph (389.4 kph)
Service Ceiling..30,200 feet (9,204.9 m)
Range..825 miles (1,327.6 km)
Crew...One

The fourth, fifth and sixth sections of Fighting Six (VF-6) fly formation near San Diego, California on 28 May 1940. The fourth section markings were Black, the fifth section was Willow Green and the sixth section had Lemon Yellow markings. Each aircraft had Mk XLIII bomb racks installed. (Tailhook Photo Service)

This F3F-2 (BuNo 0968) was assigned to the commanding officer of VF-6 and had Insignia Red section markings and a True Blue tail. The pilot's expertise in Gunnery was rewarded by the award of a Battle E. (NMNA)

F3F-2s of VMF-1 on the ramp at MCAS Quantico, Virginia. 1-MF-1 was the aircraft assigned to the unit commanding officer. The second aircraft, BuNo 1009 (1-MF-2) was originally assigned to the commanding officer. Aircraft routinely rotated to overhaul facilities, possibly explaining the reassignment of this aircraft as the second aircraft of the first section. (Sid Bradd)

The Mk XLI bomb rack was standard equipment of the F3F series of fighters. Two such racks were carried under the lower wings and were capable of carrying 110 pound bombs. The latch mechanism is in the center and the inverted U shaped items are sway braces. (Grumman)

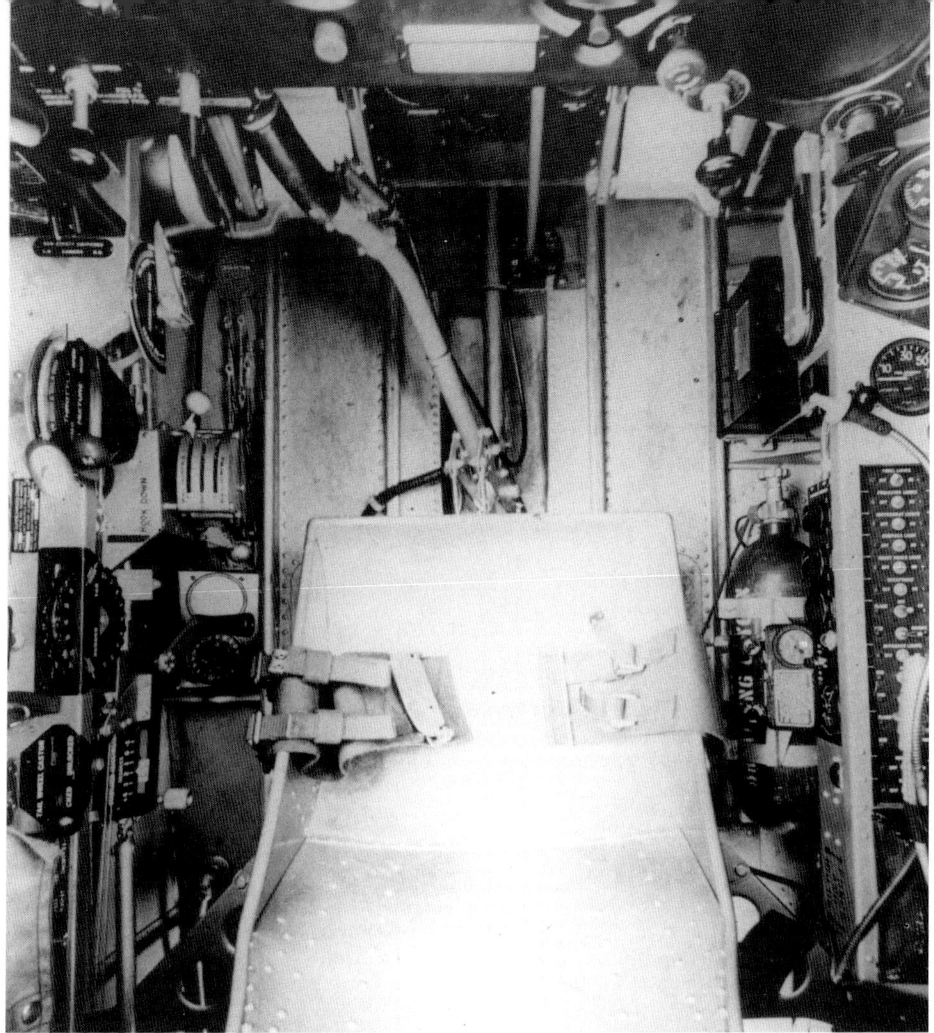

The cockpit of a F3F-2. The bottle alongside the seat is the pilot's oxygen bottle which was Green. The seat lacks a shoulder harness, although the seat belts are in place. The throttle and mixture controls are on the port bulkhead along with the tail hook control, trim wheel and propeller controls. The radio and electronics panels are on the starboard side. (Grumman)

The Mk III telescopic gun sight was used on the F3F. The ring bead sights were used for air-to-air engagements; while the telescope was used for dive bombing. (Grumman)

The port weapons bay of the F3F housed a .30 caliber machine gun and 200 rounds of ammunition. The starboard weapons bay housed a .50 caliber machine gun and 50 rounds of ammunition. The ammunition can has been partially removed from the aircraft. A blast tube extends from the gun barrel through the engine cowling. (Grumman)

The instrument panel was Black . Flight instruments were clustered on the main panel, while engine instruments were on the auxiliary panel at right. Gun charging handles are visible on either side of the main panel and the Mk III gun sight was located above the panel. Just below the panel at the left was the propeller control and fire extinguisher handles. (Grumman)

This F3F-2 (BuNo 0989) was used in the 1941 movie "Dive Bomber", where it crashed killing the hero. In reality, the F3F ended its career at the Naval Technical Training School, Jacksonville. Fred McMurray's prototype pressure suit was draped over the fuselage and the helmet was placed on the cart in the foreground. (Warner Brothers via James Farmer)

F3F's did receive camouflage finishes after Pearl Harbor in accordance with Navy directives of the time. This F3F (BuNo 0995) was Blue Gray over Light Gray with Black lettering. This aircraft was stricken from the inventory during January of 1943. (Peter M. Bowers)

(Below/Left) This F3F was painted in overall Nonspecular Light Gray in accordance with directives issued on 30 December 1940. The fuselage code was in White and a national insignia was added to the fuselage. (Larkins)

The sole surviving F3F. This F3F-2 (BuNo 0976) was recovered from the Pacific Ocean. where it had been ditched by 1st Lieutenant Robert E. Galer during 1940. Galer went on to earn the Medal of Honor for his actions as commanding officer of VMF-224, flying Wildcats on Guadalcanal. (Tailhook Photo Service)

F3F-3

In the Summer of 1938, with unanticipated difficulties occurring in both the Brewster F2A and Grumman F4F monoplane fighter programs, and with an additional carrier air group being formed for the USS WASP (CV-7), the Navy found itself facing a critical aircraft shortage. Grumman had foreseen this situation and, even before F3F-2 production was completed, had proposed a production run of "improved" F3F-2s to satisfy short range requirements for an additional fighter squadron. To this end, F3F-2 (BuNo 1031), having been already delivered to NAS Anacostia, was returned to the Bethpage plant in May of 1938 for modification; becoming the XF3F-3 prototype (BuNo 1031).

In an attempt to maximize the ultimate capabilities of the design, Grumman incorporated several aerodynamic refinements into the XF3F-3. These included a redesigned wing leading edge, a tighter fitting cowling, deletion of the fuselage cooling vents and a redesigned windshield (similar to that on the XF4F-2).

The aircraft was tested throughout the Summer of 1938, both in the Langley, Virginia, wind tunnel and later at NAS Anacostia and the Naval Aircraft Factory in Philadelphia. On 15 August, the aircraft was returned to Bethpage for installation of the upper wing of the G-32 to test the effects of flaps on the low speed performance of the aircraft. It was found that the low speed performance gains did not justify the additional weight and, on 23 August, the aircraft was again returned to Grumman for refit of the original wing and some minor modifications. It wasn't until 19 October, that the aircraft was finally delivered to NAS Anacostia for Acceptance Trials; which were completed on 14 December. Meanwhile, production was already underway with the first production aircraft (BuNo 1444) being accepted on 16 December.

Production F3F-3s did not incorporate the new XF4F-2 style canopy, instead using the same design as the production F3F-2s. Incidentally, the F3F-2 and F3F-3 were so similar in design, that they had the same Grumman design number (G-19).

The F3F-3 was equipped with a 950 hp Wright R-1820-22 Cyclone air-cooled radial engine fitted with a two-speed supercharger; which gave the aircraft a service ceiling of 30,000 feet, nearly 5,300 feet higher than the Pratt & Whitney powered F3F-1. Armament consisted of one .50 caliber machine gun and one .30 caliber machine gun mounted in the fuselage forward of the windshield and firing through the propeller arc. Two Mk XLI bomb racks were carried under each lower wing capable of carrying 110 pound bombs. A fuel capacity of 130 gallons gave the F3F-3 a range of 730 miles. Loaded weight was 4,534 pounds, but the aerodynamic refinements made to the aircraft gave it a top speed of 264 mph, some eight mph faster than the F3F-2.

Twenty-seven F3F-3s were built (BuNos 1444-1471); with a majority being assigned to VF-5 aboard USS YORKTOWN. VMF-2, VF-4 and VF-6 also received F3F-3s to augment those squadrons. Two were assigned to NAS Anacostia (BuNos 1462 and 1463). On 20 June 1941, VF-5 turned in its aircraft marking the end of Navy usage F3F-3s in front-line units. Following fleet phaseout most F3F-3s were sent to NAS Corpus Christi, Texas for use as advanced fighter-trainers. Several also went to NAS Miami, Florida, for the same purpose. Following Training Command service, most surviving airframes were assigned to Naval Technical Training Schools, primarily at NAS Norman, Oklahoma, NAS Great Lakes, Illinois, and NAS Memphis, Tennessee. No F3F-3 is known to have survived the Second World War. These graceful little aircraft have not been forgotten. Many future naval aviators first got

The XF3F-3 (BuNo 1031) at the Bethpage facility on 16 October 1938. Production F3F-3s did not incorporate the modified windshield fitted to the XF3F-3 (which was similar to that used on the XF4F-2). Production aircraft also had a more aerodynamic engine exhaust fairing. (Grumman)

interested in aviation because of men like Al Williams or by seeing the movie "Dive Bomber" with its little F3Fs in beautiful Technicolor. Talking to pilots such as Robert Galer, Milo Haines, Zeke Cormier and Tommy Blackburn, brought back stories of the Grumman biplanes that were still vivid in their memories after some fifty years. Perhaps that is the greatest tribute to be given to the Grumman biplanes.

A F3F-3 (BuNo 1642) assigned to NAS Anacostia for developmental testing. The aircraft was overall Silver with the top surface of the upper wing in Chrome Yellow. This F3F-3 was later assigned to NAS Memphis, Tennessee, before being stricken. (Jeff Ethell)

A F3F-3 (BuNo 1463) in a steep left turn. Stressed to plus nine and minus three Gs, the F3F was a very strong aircraft and the only flight limitation was intentional spins. This aircraft was one of two (BuNos 1462 & 1463) that were never assigned to a squadron, serving their active careers at NAS Anacostia, Virginia. It ended its days at Naval Technical Training School, Great Lakes, Illinois. (Grumman)

A F3F-3 (BuNo 1445) prior to delivery to VF-5 on 29 December 1938. Externally, the differences between the F3F-2 and F3F-3 were the lack of air intakes on the fuselage above the horizontal stabilizers, faired exhausts, and the lack of cooling vents on the fuselage near the cowling. The unit marking was applied incorrectly at the factory with the star pointed down instead of up. (Grumman)

VF-5 was the only fleet unit to completely re-equip with the F3F-3. These Red tailed F3F-3s fly in a vertical stack formation near NAS North Island, San Diego, California on 27 November 1939. VF-5 was assigned to USS YORKTOWN (CV-5). (Tailhook Photo Service.)

A F3F-3 (BuNo 1454) on the snow covered ramp at Grumman's Bethpage facility. The government furnished gun sight has yet to be installed. This aircraft had a Red tail and Black section markings. The aircraft was lost at sea while aboard USS YORKTOWN on 1 July 1940. (Grumman)

Due to the fact that the propeller is undamaged and the canopy is closed, the author believes that this NAS Anacostia based F3F-3 (BuNo 1463) was damaged in a wind storm, rather than a crash. (Dave Lucabaugh)

As Brewster F2As and Grumman F4Fs became available in late 1940 and early 1941, F3Fs were transferred to the Training Command. These F3F-2 and F3F-3s from NAS Miami fly a right echelon formation. The lead aircraft lacks an oil cooler fairing and it appears that the landing gear is not quite fully retracted. (Dave Lucabaugh)

G-22 (Gulfhawk II)

On 6 December 1936, Grumman delivered the only Grumman Design 22 (G-22) built to the Gulf Oil Company and it's chief pilot, Major AI Williams. Built to replace his first GULFHAWK, a Curtiss Hawk 1-A, the GULFHAWK II would go on to become the most famous of all the Grumman biplanes, thrilling millions of spectators at hundreds of air shows between 1936 and 1948, when the GULFHAWK II was replaced by what would become the last GULFHAWK, a G-58A Bearcat (F8F) known as GULFHAWK IV.

In an effort to produce an airplane with the highest possible performance, the GULFHAWK II incorporated a 1,000 hp Wright R-1820-G1 Cyclone air-cooled radial engine with the oil and fuel systems modified to permit thirty minutes of inverted flight. No military equipment was installed, resulting in an aircraft nearly 400 pounds lighter than a production F3F-2. Major Williams replaced the standard cowling with a reduced diameter cowling of his own design featuring rocker arm blisters. The carburetor intake was also moved to the rear just behind the cowling. The airframe itself was a hybrid of the F2F-1 and F3F-2. The fuselage was that of the F3F-2 series minus armament, arresting gear and increased ventral area. Total fuel capacity was 143.5 gallons in three tanks. The upper wing had the same twenty-eight foot six inch span as the F2F-1; while the vertical and horizontal tail surfaces were those of the F3F-2. The windsheild and canopy were similar to the F3F-1, but included additional bracing on the upper Plexiglas portion just above the pilot's head. Later in the aircraft's career, it was fitted with an F3F-2 style canopy and windshield. The solid rubber tailwheel used by the Navy was replaced by a larger diameter inflatable tire. The results of these modifications were impressive, since the GULFHAWK II had a maximum speed of 290 mph, 34 mph faster than a Navy F3F-2.

While an impressive airshow performer, the GULFHAWK II was also used as a research

The Gulfhawk II had F2F-1 wings with a span of twenty-eight feet six inches and the fuselage of a F3F-2. The aircraft was overall Orange with Insignia Blue and White trim. The struts, bracing and antenna masts were polished aluminum and the undersides of the horizontal stabilizers were Gloss Black. (Grumman)

platform by Gulf to test new fuels, oils, lubricants and equipment developed by Gulf and Williams. In 1938, the aircraft was shipped to England for participation in the Gatwick Airshow. Williams also flew performances in Holland, France and Germany. It was in Germany that Ernst Udet, the second ranking German ace of the First World War, with sixty-two kills, became the only other person ever to fly the GULFHAWK II. In return, Williams was permitted to fly the Messerschmitt Bf 109, the first American to do so.

As part of his aerobatic routines, Williams demonstrated the aircraft's ability to conduct "dive bombing". Al and his mechanic, Frank Tye, installed a specially designed bomblet rack capable of carrying four small black powder bomblets. A specially erected building on the airfield was filled with gas and the small charges would ignite the gas destroying the building in a ball of flame, much to the delight of the crowd.

During 1943, at the request of Army Air Forces Chief of Staff, General H. H. "Hap" Arnold, Williams toured military bases in the GULFHAWK II for three months, inspiring student aviators with his precision flight demonstrations.

On 11 October 1948, after twelve years of operation, the GULFHAWK II flew its last flight demonstration before landing at the Washington National Airport. Upon landing, the GULFHAWK II was presented to the Smithsonian Institution Nation Air Museum and, at the same time, Williams took delivery of his final GULFHAWK, a G-58A (F8F-1 Bearcat). In keeping with tradition, the G-58A was christened GULFHAWK IV. The GULFHAWK II can be seen today at the National Air & Space Museum in Washington, D.C.

The GULFHAWK II at the Grumman Farmingdale facility prior to delivery during 1936. The aircraft canopy was modified with additional bracing above the pilot's head. Later it was replaced with a F3F-2 canopy. Williams had a combination lock installed on the baggage compartment door. (Grumman)

Tailwheel

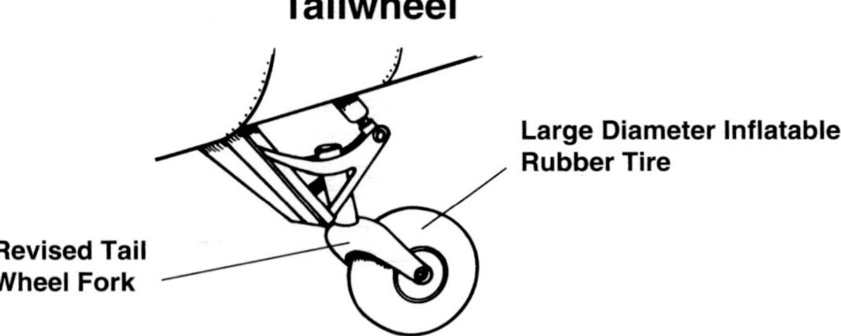

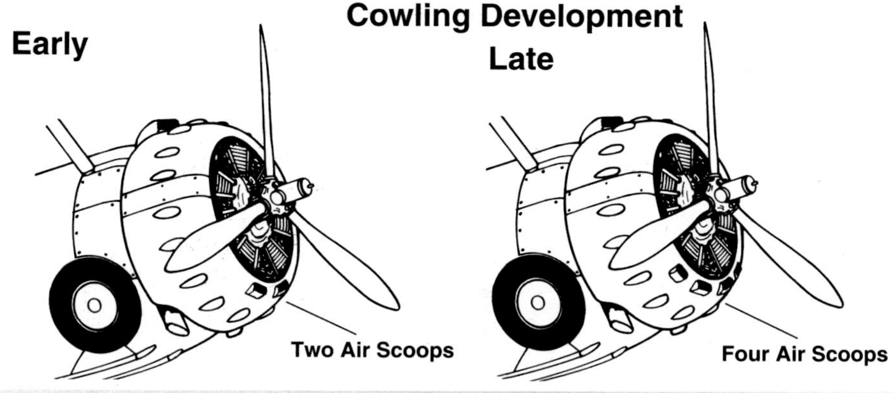

Al Williams makes a sharp pull-up from extremely low altitude during one of his flight demonstrations. During 1943, Williams toured military training bases across the U.S. to inspire student pilots to seek perfection in their flying. (Ole C. Griffith)

(Left) As part of his demonstration, Williams "dive bombed" gas filled structures on the ground. The bomblets Williams carried had a small black power charge that would ignite the gas in the structure with spectacular results. (Ole C. Griffith)

With a top speed of 290 mph, the GULFHAWK II was the fastest of the Grumman biplanes. Williams made a number of refinements to the aircraft including a close fitting cowling with rocker arm blisters and the elimination of the large oil cooler under the nose. The bomb rack for the bomblets is visible under the port wing. (Ole C. Griffith)

G-32 (Gulfhawk III/UC-103)

Nearly two years after taking delivery of the G-22 (GULFHAWK II), Al Williams took delivery of a second Grumman biplane, the Grumman Design 32 (G-32). The G-32 was delivered to Williams, chief pilot for Gulf Oil Company, on 6 May 1938, at a cost of $21,349.37.

Powered by a 1,000 hp Wright R-1820G Cyclone air-cooled radial engine , the G-32 was a two seat aircraft based on the F3F-2 airframe. As with the G-22, it was fitted with a reduced-diameter engine cowling, featuring rocker arm blisters and dual oil cooler intakes on the lower lip of the cowling. The aircraft had a maximum speed of 275 mph, twelve mph faster than the production F3F-3. It was also fitted with dual flight controls, and, surprisingly, trailing edge, split-type flaps on the upper wing just inboard of the ailerons.

Registered as NC1051, Major Williams christened the G-32 as the GULFHAWK III, the third Williams aircraft to bear the GULFHAWK title. The aircraft was painted in the same brilliant color scheme as the previous GULFHAWKS, overall Orange with Insignia Blue and White trim with polished aluminum cabane and interplane struts and horizontal stabilizer bracing.

Major Williams used the GULFHAWK III as a utility aircraft, flying passengers, making cross-country flights and as a backup for the single seat GULFHAWK II. Prior to the start of the Second World War, Gulf sold the GULFHAWK III to sport pilot Woolworth Donohue, however, in November of 1942, the aircraft was purchased by the U.S. Army Air Force for use as a utility aircraft at Bolling Field, Washington, D.C. The USAAF gave the aircraft the designation UC-103-GR (USAAF serial 42-97044). On 10 November 1943, the aircraft was sent to Homestead Army Air Field, Florida, for use as a high performance ferry pilot training aircraft.

During a training flight from Miami to Tampa, the aircraft suffered a fuel pump failure and crashed in the Everglades. The UC-103 was recovered and subsequently scrapped at Homestead AAF. Official Air Force records indicate the aircraft was "not in the inventory, no record of disposition," on 21 February 1946.

G-32

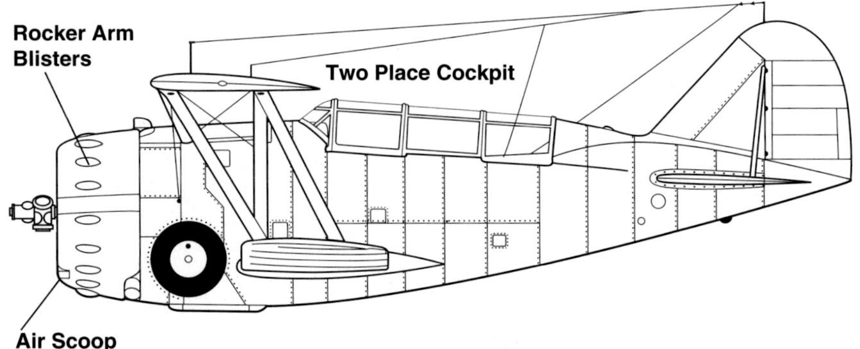

The GULFHAWK III in a hangar at Alleghany County Airport, Pennsylvania. The aircraft had an inflatable tailwheel in place of the hard tailwheel used on the F3F series. The stabilizer is in the full leading edge down position of -2.5 degrees. (Jack Binder)

The G-32 used a two piece rearward sliding canopy with a fixed center section. There are hand-holds in the upper wing center section and a combination lock on the baggage compartment door, like the one installed on the single seat G-22 GULFHAWK II. (Jack Binder)

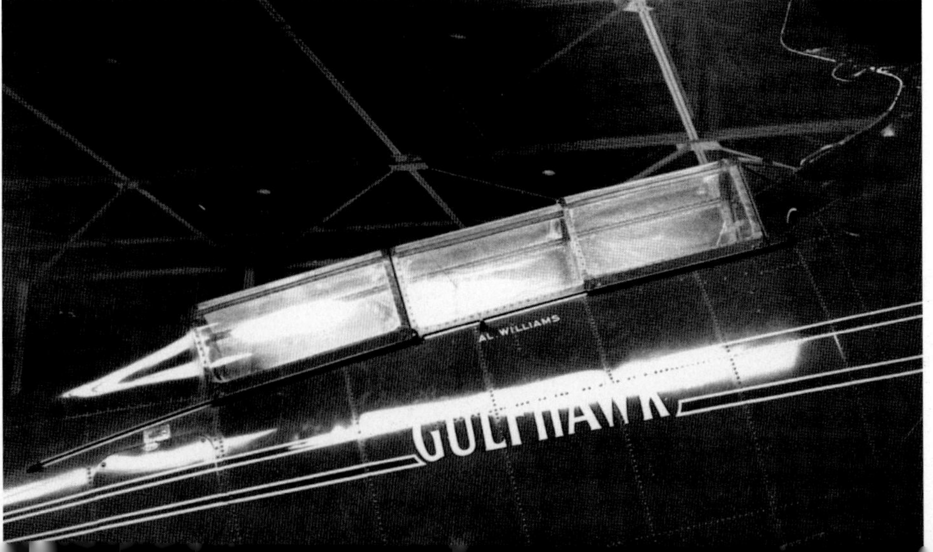

Major Al Williams poses with the GULFHAWK III. The aircraft carried the same color scheme as the G-22 GULFHAWK II demonstration aircraft. The G-32 became part of the U.S. Army Air Force inventory during November of 1942, under the designation UC-103. (Grumman)

The GULFHAWK III used a large inflatable tailwheel that was semi-retrated in to the fuselage. The aircraft had a top speed of 275 mph, some twelve mph faster than a production F3F-2 fighter. (Grumman)

Major WIlliams runs up the GULFHAWK III; while still in the chocks. The forward fuselage upper decking was much more aerodynamic; since it did not have the weapons bay bulges and machine gun troughs. The upper wing was fitted with split trailing edge flaps inboard of the ailerons. (Grumman)

Major Al Williams and Sam Pryor in the GULFHAWK III at Roosevelt Field. The rear cockpit of the GULFHAWK III was fitted with full instruments and dual flight controls. The two sliding canopies were connected by a fixed center section. (Grumman)

G-32A

A third and final civilian variant of the F3F series was built, the G-32A. Nearly identical to her sister ship, the G-32, the G-32A was retained by the Grumman Corporation as a demonstrator.

The G-32A was a two seat aircraft powered by a 950 hp Wright R-I820G Cyclone air-cooled radial. Like the G-32, the G-32A was fitted with two independent rearward sliding canopies and dual flight controls. The aircraft also featured a blistered cowling, split flaps on the upper wing and an inflatable tailwheel. Fuel capacity was 130 gallons, giving the aircraft a maximum range of 700 nautical miles. Dual oil cooler air intakes were located on the lower lip of the engine cowling.

Although externally similar to the G-32, there were several differences between the two aircraft. Most noticeable of these was the small triangular ventral fin immediately below the rudder. Other minor differences included two fresh air inlets located just above the leading edge of the horizontal stabilizers. These inlets were used to reduce carbon monoxide seepage into the cockpits. Also, four louvers were added to two access panels on the fuselage immediately behind the engine cowling; which were used for accessory cooling.

Following the G-32 off the production line, the G-32A was retained by Grumman and delivered on 1 July 1938. Registered as NC1326, the G-32A was also known as "The Red Ship", since the aircraft was painted overall Red with Black and White trim. Grumman used the aircraft for demonstration and utility purposes and also as a camera platform to photograph other Grumman aircraft. On occasion, it was flown by the founder of Grumman, Leroy Grumman. Grumman owned and operated the aircraft until November of 1942, when the USAAF obtained the aircraft, and designated it as the UC-103 (AAF serial 42-97045). Air Force history cards indicate that the aircraft was sent to Homestead Army Air Field on 10 November 1943 as one of thirty-three aircraft delivered to the Caribbean Wing of the Ferrying Command. From there it was sent to the 1st Staff Squadron, Headquarters USAAF, at Bolling

G-32

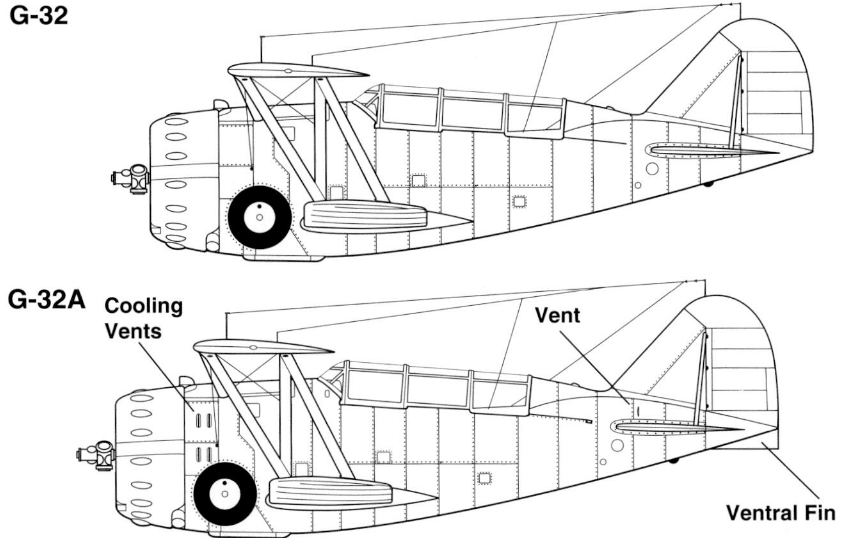

G-32A Cooling Vents

Grumman test pilot S. A. "Connie" Converse and New York Daily Mirror reporter Georgette Meyer pose along side the Grumman G-32A demonstrator at the Bethpage plant during June of 1938. The G-32A was painted overall "Cornell" Red, while the fuselage stripe, cabane and interplane struts, wing roots and wing leading edges were Black. The wing leading edge and fuselage stripe were also outlined in White. (Grumman)

Army Air Field, Washington D.C., on 9 December 1943. It remained at Bolling until being declared surplus on 27 January 1945.

After being declared surplus, the aircraft was purchased by civilian pilot Clayton Long, the first of six civilian owners between 1945 and 1971. Immediately after the war, the aircraft was registered as NC46110 and it retained this registration until Ben Bradley restored the aircraft during 1962. In 1954, the aircraft showed up at a Rockford, Illinois, airshow painted overall Black with Red cabane and interplane struts, cowling blisters and a large diagonal Red

Connie Converse and Georgette Meyer return from a flight in which Meyer claimed to be the first woman to fly faster than 400 mph. To reach this speed, the G-32A had to enter a vertical dive. (Grumman)

The G-32A at Rockford, Illinois during 1954. The aircraft was owned by Ben Bradley, who owned it twice, from 1947-1948 and again from 1949 to 1966. The aircraft was overall Black with Red cowling blisters, struts, elevators and rudder. The diagonal stripe was Red and the rudder trim tab was Black. The circle on the tail was the Grumman logo. (Seybel/Grumman)

stripe on the fuselage. The elevators and rudder were also Red.

Following Ben Bradley's restoration in 1962, the aircraft was painted to resemble a F3F-2, and, while being very colorful, the scheme was highly inaccurate. The aircraft retained this scheme up until 7 August 1971, when the aircraft was destroyed after an inflight fire. The pilot and passenger both bailed out and survived. There were several salvageable parts and these formed the basis of an essentially "new build" G-32A.

This "new" G-32A was one of four aircraft (one G-32A and three F3F-2s) manufactured by the Texas Aircraft Factory of Fort Worth, Texas. All four aircraft are airworthy, and all four aircraft have been delivered to their new owners. With these aircraft, the population of Grumman biplane fighters had grown to seven as of 1996!

The author and the "new build" G-32A prior to painting in 1993. This aircraft is currently owned by Cinema Air Inc, of Carlsbad, California. The aircraft differs from its original configuration in having a smooth cowling and oil cooler fairing under the nose. The aircraft was overall Chromate Green and Silver Dope. (Jerry Foster)

The G-32A at the Grumman Bethpage facility on 1 June 1967. The late Bill Ross owned the aircraft at this time. Following Ben Bradley's restoration in 1962, the G-32A was painted to represent a F3F. The section markings were Green and the tail surfaces were Red. The squadron insignia was for VF-5 and the fictitious BuNo was actually Grumman's construction number for the G-32A (447). (Grumman)

The G-32A and one of three F3F-2s built share the Cinema Air Jet Center ramp at Palomar Airport in Carlsbad, California. Cinema Air owns the G-32A and two of the F3F-2s while the Lone Star Flight Museum of Galveston, Texas owns the other F3F-2. The California aircraft are painted in the markings of VF-7 aboard USS WASP, but do not conform to the Navy's system of markings and numbering. Additionally, VF-7 never flew F3F-2s, being equipped with F3F-1s instead. (Dick Martin)

49

U.S. Navy Fighters
of the Second World War
in Action From

squadron/signal publications